Active

Listening

Practical Skills for Effective Communication

(Essential Keys to Effective Communication in Relationships)

Roxann Londono

Published By **Ryan Princeton**

Roxann Londono

Active Listening: Practical Skills for Effective Communication (Essential Keys to Effective Communication in Relationships)

ISBN   978-1-998927-50-0

Legal & Disclaimer

The information contained in this book is not designed to replace or take the place of any form of medicine or professional medical advice. The information in this book has been provided for educational & entertainment purposes only.

The information contained in this book has been compiled from sources deemed reliable, and it is accurate to the best of the Author's knowledge; however, the Author cannot guarantee its accuracy and validity and cannot be held liable for any errors or omissions. Changes are periodically made to this book. You must consult your doctor or get professional medical advice before using any of the suggested remedies, techniques, or information in this book.

Table Of Contents

Chapter 1: Listening With Empathy Can Improve Your Life

Have you ever questioned how a few humans appear to be successful so without issues in such a lot of unique strategies?

In school, they weren't the splendid searching human beings in each crowd, however they had friends and dates.

In college, they may no longer have seemed especially studious, but they had been given the pinnacle grades.

If their jobs comprise selling anything, they don't look or sound like salesmen, but they near income to the most difficult customers.

If their jobs comprise taking orders, they're favorites with manipulate and customers. Sometimes they're special favorites with customers who otherwise in reality seem to love being advocate.

If their jobs comprise fitness care, they're the ones who've never been sued.

If their jobs contain politics, they're probably to choose to be professionals as opposed to applicants, however they might flow as a long manner as they want to transport.

If they have to have a examine new method capabilities, or maybe new languages, they might do this.

If they have got kids, they're possibly even to have higher relationships with their youngsters than distinct humans appear to have.

And plenty of them don't even need remedy to preserve wholesome blood strain tiers.

On closer exam, it's no longer surely that those human beings have continuously had all the suitable notable fortune in lifestyles. In fact a variety of them have survived sad childhoods, with abusive parent-figures, infection or incapacity inside the family, contamination or disability in their non-public, or a couple of of those topics. Those tough times may additionally moreover have contributed to their grownup success...Due to the truth seeking to make the excellent of hard times can train youngsters to pay near interest to others.

What those human beings have in common is they've determined to pay attention.

Let's begin with an knowledge that "listening," on this e-book, consists of extra than simply taking note of. Obviously maximum parents are most aware of the spoken phrases we hear while we pay interest. Obviously paying attention to impairment makes listening greater hard. Nevertheless, partial listening to loss motivates some humans to listen greater attentively, and fashionable deafness motivates some human beings to pay closer attention to opportunity sorts of verbal exchange. People who don't pay interest spoken phrases the least bit use some of the identical skills every person else uses on the equal time as we pay attention with empathy. So, regardless of the fact that this e-book isn't about any of the techniques people seize up on precise sorts and levels of taking note of loss, this ebook does use "listening" to encompass all of the techniques we gather information from others. Deaf people like dancer Heather Whitestone may be said to "pay interest" with the useful resource of studying, looking, and feeling vibrations. The advantages of listening are available to them too.

Listening makes us adorable.

While a few listeners are shy, particularly whilst more youthful, and find out it hard to get a verbal exchange going with awesome listeners, listeners are irresistibly appealing to talkers. The impact is so robust that Margaret Kent provided a cash-again assure: If any girl may want to show that she'd supplied a replica of How to Marry the Man of Your Choice, at the same time as it have become a brand new e-book, and after following its instructions for two years she changed into no longer married to the man or woman of her choice, she have to claim cash decrease back. The ebook gave suggestions on such things as choosing a capability husband, dressing properly, and making up after a quarrel, however its advice to readers who had found an eligible prospect became: Listen. One phase changed into headed "How to Listen Your Way Into a Man's Heart."

Male reviewers resented the concept that they might be so smooth to get, however men who approached Margaret Kent's e-book with an expertise of psychology placed it clean to concentrate their way into ladies's hearts, too. Indeed some authors advise that humans restriction the length of taking note of people they don't intend to marry, for humanitarian motives.

Listening boosts university students' test scores.

With its attention on analyzing, the traditional college machine gives a stated gain to university students with well evolved language competencies. Listening, that is much less frequently formally studied than reading, writing, and speaking, gives a clean advantage.

It's been claimed that "commonplace adult guys assume with their eyes, commonplace girls assume with their fingers, and 'proficient' university students assume with their ears." This oversimplified view of the concept of sensory mode choice resonates with enough people's enjoy to benefit a fuller speak later. In this creation, permit's conform to apprehend that listening with empathy engages all 3 of our number one senses. Good university college college students watch teachers' faces for brought records; additionally they write down notes on the lecture. "Listening" with eyes and hands, in addition to ears, allows us absorb and maintain greater facts, and furthermore builds that pleasant feel of rapport humans enjoy on the same time as they're getting to the same element, using the identical sensory channels. The feel of rapport encourages teachers (and audio system, singers, actors, and all performers) to enjoy better, reputation more really, and generally supply higher shows. Even despite the fact that actual teachers' "liking" of character college students isn't allowed to have an effect on their grading manner, college college students who pay interest actively and empathetically get a better top notch of education.

Listening improves earnings performance.

There are instances at the same time as, if a prospective patron and issuer are speakme properly, what they apprehend and agree on is that the vendor doesn't want a product. Good profits techniques restriction those sad moments with the useful resource of making sure the income employees make investments their efforts in selling only topics the clients do want to shop for.

When it's worthwhile for a enterprise to make income and advertising and marketing and marketing complete-time jobs, the purpose of a advertising and marketing and marketing and advertising and marketing advertising and marketing advertising marketing campaign may be to locate people looking for merchandise/offerings. Deep discounts on popular products can artwork to keep greater humans into range of the real marketing and advertising strive or truely to dispose of overstocked objects earlier than their "promote with the aid of manner of" date, and sponsorship of famous community occasions like sports activities sports and bazaars can be some component the successful business owner enjoys too— however a achievement corporation proprietors do not forget these as tactics to discover and meet the small corporation of folks who are within the marketplace for his or her more worthwhile merchandise. How do they realise who the ones people are and the way to attraction to them? Once successful marketers are inside fashion of folks that might be prospective customers, they pay attention.

Listening improves enterprise ratings.

Obviously, understanding the instructions we're given makes it much less hard to conform with them. There are, however, folks that appear to experience being hard to delight. Are they merely miserable, generally awful, those who enjoy venting their unwell feeling on others, or are they individuals who experience a moral obligation to apply money to "reward pinnacle and correct evil"? Empathetic listeners not quality recognize the distinction, however obtain the rewards of fascinating those tough customers who probable wouldn't discover being so tough this kind of treasured method within the event that they weren't in a role accessible out beneficiant rewards.

Listening improves the fine of fitness care.

It also can appear that some scientific scientific medical doctors in recent times do all that they will to avoid listening, to reduce touch with sufferers and cognizance absolutely on lab tests. Tests do provide goal evidence of the existence of a treatable condition and the improvement of treatment. However, even a hectic MD will find that patients and body of personnel are more a success in carrying out remedy plans while the doctor listens to them and makes certain they understand the remedy plans.

Practical nurses, therapists, and unique lower-ranked health care providers are from time to time accused of trying treatments beyond their qualifications when they want to deliver patients to the MD or maybe to a expert. This accusation is observed even if country wide clinical offerings eliminate the economic impediment from consulting a practitioner at the right stage of information. What nurses and therapists regularly describe is the effect of docs not taking the time to pay attention to patients who can also seem to be rambling incoherently or honestly absorbing interest.

A 22-yr-antique masseuse's tale is typical: "The affected character came in for a decrease lower back rub and stated a 'slipped disc' inside the lumbar vicinity. In fact the L4 vertebra was protruding abnormally. Of course I instructed her she need to cancel her appointment with me and visit a medical health practitioner or chiropractor. She reached back and grabbed my hands, leaned her lumbar region in opposition to them, and stated 'Just push!' Luckily this affected person turned into one of these people who have loose ligaments, usually, and whose bones do 'pop' inside and outside of joint without hassle. She felt L4 snap once more into its place and desired to proceed collectively collectively together with her once more massage. I gave a moderate, 'first do no harm' rubdown on the same time as we stated her all over again harm and the other, greater essential problems that could had been present. She didn't receive as authentic with she had any excessive problems however, after the again rub, she did time desk a test-up with a clinical medical doctor."

Practical nurses, psychotherapists, rub down therapists, chiropractors, and bodily therapists who workout out of doors a health facility do see patients who like attention. By listening, however, they could once in a while recognize early signs and symptoms of a actual disorder in the various rambling and interest-searching out. A patient who feels established via way of a practitioner's listening can be much more likely to get the actual disorder, if one is gift, diagnosed and dealt with.

Listening builds credibility...For political applicants, specialists, managers, teachers, or every person else.

In 1991, the controversial, a outstanding deal criticized governor of a as a substitute small State, this is extensively appeared as corrupt, rarely seemed just like the satisfactory desire to run closer to a well-known incumbent. In fact many Americans credit rating rating the presence of a spoiler candidate for the election of Bill Clinton as President in 1992, and muckraking newshounds credit rating corruption for his reelection as governor, however why did his birthday party even nominate the huge, awkward greater youthful guy with the scratchy voice? Bill Clinton's mystery political weapon have become the non-public attraction an powerful listener responsibilities. Though criticized for letting himself be distracted through a high-quality type of younger woman, President Clinton impressed guys and older girls as "a honestly pleasant, likable fellow": "His eyes slight up, and he makes you revel in as if you were the nice one in that crowded room."

When the Clintons got here to Washington, they modified severa federal personnel, from politically appointed "communications officials" to profession authorities employees who belief their jobs had been "non-political," with greater younger humans, which includes a number of the youngest human beings ever appointed to their positions. This arguable go with the flow paid off because the manipulate's use of those more younger humans's electricity and ingenuous appeal have emerge as apparent. To a exceptional amount Dee Myers, George Stephanopoulos, and dozens of an entire lot an awful lot much less well-known colleagues have become the "ears" the Clintons used to keep being attentive to the man in the street, after safety troubles stored Bill Clinton from meeting the man in the road for my part. Everyone in Washington, on the side of the college university college students and maximum of the tourists, turn out to be chatted up via one or more human beings in the Clinton White House. Despite livid controversy approximately Bill Clinton's universal performance, his secondhand listening received him a second time period.

Empathetic listening certainly comes a whole lot much less clearly to Donald Trump, even though it's a potential he's labored tough to look at. President Trump, like Boris Johnson, often fails to enchantment folks that see each man inside the records media or in some unspecified time in the future of a crowded room. People who meet both the President or the Prime Minister in my opinion, but,

14

normally document that they may be "exceedingly pleasant" in man or woman. (People who dislike them grumble that a similar listening technique worked for Adolf Hitler.) Though regularly taken into consideration abrasive after they do more talking than listening, each Trump and Johnson have carefully studied their audiences and selected their speakme elements based absolutely mostly on what their audiences need them to mention.

You don't need to be a flesh presser to apply the listening method to strong your profession. Listening competencies worked for the Clinton manage's battalion of more youthful, difficult to understand, junior federal employees, together with quiet, personal White House building personnel and extremely-personal protection body of workers, as well as for the Clintons themselves. Though some Clinton staffers took unfair quantities of blame for the administration's unpopular moves, now that the unpleasantness is in the back of them they're not among the getting old Americans now grumbling about being "kicked upstairs" or pushed into early retirement.

Listening allows adults to examine new "languages."

If you need to speak each other language "like a community," it's already too past due: the brain's ability to obtain "nearby fluency" in a language declines fast after age five. As an grownup you may, but, examine to talk correctly in a brand new language, with excellent enough of an accessory to amuse pals. You can observe new laptop structures' or social media's "languages," too, and almost every different challenge skills that could come to be useful. How can adults test new languages and different talents, that is what our brains usually do early in early life? By turning into childlike—eager to check, willing to make an occasional mistake—and listening.

Listening improves circle of relatives relationships.

Children's private potential to take a look at language and social talents is caused via the quantity of time adults spend paying attention to them, even at the child-babble diploma. (Psychologists now say that imitating infant-babble is beneficial even as toddlers are in reality beginning to growth manipulate of the noises they make, although counterproductive after infants start to talk nicely.) Of direction children moreover want to take a look at that there are instances when adults have extra on their minds than the tales children make up approximately their toys, and on occasion even the reviews children make on their stories at university or play agencies. Still, the greater actual communique with adults youngsters get, the extra easily they check the conversation skills they may use for the duration of life. That technique better take a look at ratings, better educational possibilities, and greater possibilities for achievement in higher paid careers.

It moreover approach better family relationships between dad and mom and their college-aged, teenaged, or young-individual kids. While no longer anything appears to assure that a child will document illegal drug activity, sexual "experiments," or bullying in vicinity of take part in it, time and again psychologists tell us that youngsters who report are individuals who speak with their mother and father every day, and kids who take part have a tendency to be the children of remote, authoritarian, or recklessly permissive mother and father. (Sometimes recklessly permissive mother and father do be aware of their kids, however they fail to gather the unstated meta-messages kids deliver when they want steerage or supervision.)

Listening lowers blood stress.

It's a scientific reality: When people concentrate attentively, their blood pressure lowers to or toward healthful degrees. When people communicate, or "listen" absolutely prolonged sufficient to get their danger to talk, their blood strain rises. For wholesome people this upward push in blood stress is brief and inside the ordinary variety. For hypertensive patients, it is able to pass lower lower again into the danger location. Anyone diagnosed with persistent hypertension, arteriosclerosis, atherosclerosis, or any type of "coronary coronary heart disease" can advantage from a each day exercising of attentive listening. This is probably the number one mechanism through which being married to their specific (or prolonged-time period) companions allows cardiovascular patients continue to exist.

If listening has a majority of these benefits, you can ask, why do only a few human beings appear to be playing the blessings?

Listening is a discovered talent. We all growth it to a point; anybody use it, and get the advantages of using it, to a degree, every day. However, there are tactics to enhance the effectiveness of our everyday listening conduct beyond the ordinary everyday diploma.

Chapter 2: How We Listen with Empathy

As the examples of its advantages have counseled, listening with empathy may be an excessive revel in. This isn't always normally a hassle; in maximum conditions it's easy to control the intensity. In reality, you probably already do this. What this phase can educate you is a manner to be extra aware about a few factor you already do.

However, at the same time as you start to exercising listening with a higher degree of empathy, you may discover it hard. This is ordinary. As a running closer to psycholinguist, Suzette Haden Elgin stated that it's nearly not possible to pay interest with whole interest, maximal empathy, for extra than half an hour at a time. And that's not all lousy; that degree of hobby might be overwhelming for the opportunity character, too.

Sometimes it's better to lower the extent of empathy and emotional intimacy, specifically in situations of battle that would beautify into embarrassment or possibly physical danger. Sometimes a person who is manifestly searching out a combat may be extra pissed off in recent times, and plenty an awful lot less sorry in some time, if others restrict conversation with him to discovered letters.

Hypertensive people, especially men who enlarge "anger dependancy" (a mild physical dependancy to the hormone surge associated with venting anger), typically want to avoid listening with empathy to people expressing anger. Whether those humans are tempted to charge out and counterattack the individual that harm a chum's emotions, or to lash decrease once more at the person who's indignant at them, allowing their anger to accumulate is possibly to do them greater harm than they do to others. For them, it could be useful to opposite the stairs, stated right here, for increasing empathy and intimacy. Becoming a tough man or woman's new superb friend is not their pinnacle precedence...As a minimal, now not inside the moment when the person is being difficult.

Most humans, however, have instinctively decided out that the relaxation of the arena isn't always constantly prepared for the volume of emotional intimacy and depth which have been involved while we had been gaining knowledge of to talk.

Major changes take location in our brains spherical age four to 6. Now that those adjustments are inside the returned folks, it's clean to miss the depth with which we communicated with adults at the equal time as we decided to speak.

One purpose why Helen Keller's Story of My Life remains well-known is that Keller's learning to talk changed into no longer on time long enough that she became able to describe that depth to adults.

As infants, we knew specific humans were the usage of terms to speak. We preferred very a whole lot an extremely good way to apply terms too. At first, while we had no green manner to examine new terms, we groped approximately frantically for some way to crack the code. Later on, whilst we located out the words to use for max of the topics we desired, studying a current phrase proper here and there generated less emotion.

The adults who spent most time with us— almost usually our mothers, on occasion certainly one of a kind human beings too— preferred to educate us phrases nearly as a tremendous deal as we desired to analyze phrases. Adults found it useful to interpret the first noises we made, "ma-ma," "pa-pa," as phrases of kinship that intended them.

We learned that repeating "ma-ma" brought us hobby: Mama's face searching at lovingly down at ours as she tenderly requested us what we desired. Mama gobbled our little one faces together collectively together with her eyes as she moved her mouth to expose us the manner to form greater sounds.

Then she hastened to deliver subjects we might have been attempting whilst we located out how to mimic a legitimate that resembled a word Mama used. As English-talking babies we have been pleased to find out that "wa-wa" turned into close to sufficient to get us water, "num-num" have been given us a few detail to chew at the identical time as our tooth were developing in, "ho-mee" were given us snuggled, and so forth. Mama modified into pleased, too, and so had been Daddy and Sissy and Nana, due to the reality they were keen to pay interest us say what we wanted in terms in location of scream till we either were given what we favored or fell asleep.

Our first actual recollections of talking, consequently, are reminiscences of extraordinarily empathetic listening with excessive interest and emotions of love.

Some authors may moreover have projected even greater emotion onto this affection, and the disappointment we felt that everyone inside the worldwide didn't share it, than we certainly felt at the time. When toddlers pick out up some thing they may be capable of convey and shove it into Mama's hand, Mama stays likely to bend down within the route of them, beaming motherly love, and enunciate cautiously, "Thank you for the block! Thank you for the toothbrush! Thank you for the cold boiled egg!" Funnily sufficient, even Daddy may not participate on this first-class recreation to the amount of thanking a little one for pressing a piece of cold boiled egg into his hand; Mr. Wilson round the corner became likely to shout "Go away."

So, after mastering to talk and pay attention with whole interest and hundreds of affection, we subsequent located out to imitate the manner human beings speak once they're willing to provide heaps a great deal much less hobby and affection.

Though probably too more younger to experience some thing just like the mixture of affection and exasperation with which Mr. Wilson stated "Go away," we located to mimic the general manner he said "Go away" as we found out to mention things like "Go'way" and "'Top it" and "No!" Many folks spent a long time walking in the direction of pronouncing those things as we determined out that human beings weren't possibly to obey us as fast as they preferred us to obey them.

That "Run alongside and play, infant, I'm busy" mode of communication have end up the one maximum humans use maximum of the time. We pay attention enough that we usually pay interest the phrases, however we don't usually be aware of the entire sentence or don't forget the communique.

Sometimes our respond to what we heard doesn't make revel in within the context of what some other individual stated, due to the truth we answered to handiest part of their perception.

It may be beneficial if, in region of postulating (as some writers did within the Eighties) that we reduce off communique in this way due to the fact we were so terribly harm through Mr. Wilson next door now not thanking us for handing him leftover bits of boiled egg, we postulate that we discovered to restriction the emotional intensity of our conversation due to the truth typically setting as an lousy lot strength into conversation as a little one does might be hard. We positioned that, as soon as we'd discovered out a few dozen of the most beneficial phrases, we need to talk many things with out even having to look up from what we had been doing to have a take a look at a person else's face. This become less tough and greater green.

Often it still is extra efficient to speak with minimal empathy. When we pay for groceries or take the bus to artwork, we're not searching out emotional intimacy with the cashier or the bus riding pressure.

For severa us, waving a bus pass or setting the groceries at the counter is all the conversation we need. We favor to carry out the ones transactions without searching at or talking to the alternative person involved.

(If you're one of the folks who do need the bus motive strain or the passengers to speak to you, it'd be a terrific concept to workout saying "Please, I'm a lonely needy person and I'd like a chunk interest," in preference to the "Why are YOU so UNFRIENDLY?" ordinary you may have found inside the beyond. Most people don't crave interest as desperately as you apparently do.)

However, it's useful to go once more and remember how we determined out those one in all a type modes of communication while we do want to speak with more empathy.

Now that your brain is capable of feeling empathy within the grown-up experience, as a infant's mind isn't, all you really need to do is be a part of this grownup feeling with the sooner memories of the manner you used to speak with complete interest.

You've observed out the skills; now you can select even as and the manner to use them.

To do this, it could be useful to recognition on unique factors of mom-and-child communique. Most people routinely reintroduce those elements, efficaciously, to our verbal exchange fashion in some intimate verbal exchange situations—courtship, or talking to babies. By thinking about them consciously we are able to pick out to feature them to communication with one among a type adults at the same time as it's appropriate. Here are seven standard categories of processes we are capable of pay interest with greater empathy.

1. Look at the man or woman; make eye touch...Mindfully enough to recognize while to save you.

There is, as Nancy Friday discovered, a "look" human beings have once they're pleasantly excited thru looking at distinct people. The university college students of the eyes dilate; that's why, even to people who are in love with a person who has light blue eyes, "darkish eyes" sound extra exciting than "moderate eyes." Pale blue eyes briefly look darkish when they're adoring and provoking a infant who's studying to speak. This appearance can't be faked, despite the fact that confusion about it's miles capable to show human beings who have dark eyes to lots of hopeful but false assumptions. If your eyes don't "mild up," due to this darken, while you test a difficult customer or bored scholar, they don't. Not first-rate can not anything beneficial be carried out approximately this, however someone who has "bloodless grey eyes" can also have a bonus, keeping interest in others's reactions to a product from being incorrect for a completely precise shape of interest.

Prolonged eye contact can heighten our interest in a verbal exchange, or within the exclusive person. That could make eye touch experience thrilling or alarming to a few people. However, cultural pointers normally dictate the amount of eye contact humans are expected to preserve. Each family is to a point its non-public subculture, so in demographic groups that normalize extended eye contact, humans grow up being attentive to both "Look at me when I speak to you" and

"Don't stare," from the same elders, schooling them to maintain eye contact for a advantageous common amount of seconds at a time.

Interestingly, in cultures that expect as plenty eye contact as most "Anglo" cultures do, a minority of human beings word that assembly the demand for eye touch does now not always contain in reality seeing the opportunity person's eyes the least bit.

When we appearance in the path of someone's face, regardless of how plenty that character rhapsodizes about the eyes being the windows of the soul, that individual can't tell whether eye contact has been made.

If you had been added up to feel that prolonged eye contact is competitive and impolite, you could interest at the nostril or brow of the person that thinks she or he isn't being heard if eye touch is damaged.

Some people who are capable of artwork and stroll round with out glasses frequently discover themselves assembly their cultures' goals for eye contact via looking at the part of a indistinct human-normal blur in which the face is probably to be. People who're nearsighted (like Hillary Clinton) or farsighted (like a majority of human beings over age 60) don't continuously see the eyes of individuals who experience that they're looking at those humans's "souls."

People with astigmatism, who can see moderately properly at any distance however whose eyes might also moreover additionally take numerous seconds to trade consciousness between distances, can actually increase up familiar with not clearly seeing precise human beings's eyes surely sufficient to take a look at their coloration at some level in the everyday duration of eye contact for their manner of life.

Whatever your non-public experience with eye contact has been, for the purpose of listening with empathy it's vital to take word that others whose eyes you would probably see as "staring" or "shifty" are probable to have discovered distinct tips than you located. You can check this hypothesis by way of staring once more at a person who you bear in mind you studied stares too prolonged, or looking a ways from someone who breaks eye contact first, with out otherwise changing your communication. If every of you have been searching to talk proper will using notable guidelines, a mild trade within the length of eye contact can be a bonding enjoy.

It additionally may be, truly, a lifesaving experience. Despite enhancements in understanding of cultural variations, there are nonetheless judges who will believe a person is devious and consequently accountable of a crime if the individual doesn't maintain eye contact so long as they do, and additionally judges who will accept as true with someone is aggressive, impolite, and therefore accountable of against the law if the character holds eye contact longer than they do.

(Does eye contact propose honesty or dishonesty? Sometimes it does, even as it's in evaluation with to the character's everyday behavior. People who don't habitually tell lies, however are telling one now, generally reduce or keep away from eye contact even as mendacity. People who do habitually inform lies, and are telling one now, usually preserve eye touch longer while lying.

Eye moves can will let you understand whether or not a member of the family is lying, however due to the fact you don't recognize each how lengthy a stranger normally holds eye contact nor whether or not a stranger habitually tells lies, eye movements can misinform you about a stranger who's lying. The voice is more reliable: normal liars hardly ever attain keeping the pitch of their voice from growing after they're telling lies. Either manner, versions among people' baselines are regular; surprising deviations from an character's baseline are what to look out for.)

2. Try to in shape the rhythm of your respiratory to the rhythm of the speaker's breathing.

When humans breathe at the equal rate, the first give up result is commonly that they find out it much less complex to move at similar paces and communicate on comparable pitches. They "reflect" frame moves in a subtle, subconscious manner that builds rapport, without consciously mimicking each different in an obvious manner that builds annoyance.

This may be the vital thing to communication with that "difficult" boss or patron, as an instance, who is probable to be aggravated with the useful resource of the idea that distinct people's unique tempo or pitch method they don't recognize how essential a activity is. Matching the alternative man or woman's stage of electricity tells empathetic listeners whether to shout, "Yessir, we're walking on it as rapid as we're able to!" or murmur "Of path, we're taking care to ensure we get this proper."

It moreover can be useful in spotting (and supporting) a clinical problem. If it's actually painful to respire as slowly as a person does, due to the truth the character pauses for a second or more among inhaling and exhaling, you'll be talking to a hypothyroid affected individual.

If it's extraordinarily stressful to respire as rapid as someone does, you may be speaking to a hypertensive affected person. In each case, it's nicely certainly worth seeking to healthy those humans's breath fees for as long as you could undergo, then little by little modulate back toward regular. This doesn't continually work; at the same time as it does paintings, it can assist the affected character avoid a scientific emergency.

3. Mindfully test the speaker's "frame language," however don't be distracted via way of it.

The body can't lie. Unfortunately for people who would possibly opt to "examine faces" instead of pay attention to phrases, the frame can go off undertaking rely. Glaring disparities amongst terms and "body language" can suggest that the terms aren't actual; this is a stable assumption to make if the phrases are some aspect like "This is the fine deal you'll ever discover" or "I'm always extremely joyful to exchange plans on the same day." When there's no obvious purpose to trust that the words aren't right, it's likely that the body is "speakme" about some body tool, like digestion, that the speaker isn't interested in discussing.

People who increase essential intellectual contamination regularly display apparent disparities among terms and "frame language." So do humans with persistent physical illnesses. There's a not unusual issue: maximum vital highbrow disorders are persistent physical troubles for which the number one signs and symptoms seem to consist of the mind...And persistent physical problems commonly have some impact on emotional moods, too.

If you're providing health care, it's always appropriate to direct hobby to unexpected body movements and ask what a affected person is feeling. In unique conditions, it's normally not.

four. Assume that what you pay hobby is actual, and try to don't forget what it may probably be actual of.

At this diploma of communication you're trying to see topics from the speaker's factor of view. The speaker's difficulty of view will now not typically be really unacceptable; few people in fact stay in a intellectual global for which fact statements like "All ladies, Black human beings, Italians, etc., are dumb animals whose opinions, if any, need to be systematically crushed out of them" are right. More likely it's certainly first rate from yours—on a key component.

"Driving to paintings is ordinary; the best cause not to rent a person who could have a day by day strain of an hour or greater in every path is that the individual might in all likelihood prevent the gadget the day a task inside the direction of home have become available."

"Driving to artwork is a critical ecological trouble; if a person who can be informed to do the mission lives inside walking distance, that's the character we need to hire."

When we concentrate with empathy, we permit our minds absorb the way special people's ideals and charge judgments relate to their choices and disagreements with us. Having this statistics will, in due time, help us pick out a manner (if there may be one) to kingdom our characteristic just so the other individual is of the equal opinion with it.

People don't usually recognize a difference amongst pointing out a function in order that a person else can accept as true with it, and misrepresenting that function. Mindfulness permits right right here. Suppose the alternative man or woman expresses help for a candidate you oppose.

"I'm going to vote for Candidate X too!" is a misrepresentation.

"Candidate X appears to enchantment to Group Y," or "How do you believe X's plan for Z will work over the subsequent ten years?", or maybe "X has this kind of bright, hopeful-searching smile!" are subjects you may say in a bland, supportive tone in an effort to deliver the individual an possibility to mention some thing with which you would possibly in all likelihood agree, or lead into an opportunity for you to mention something with which the person might also additionally agree.

However, listening with empathy calls for power of thoughts. Your thoughts will need to take in some phrases, then soar in advance in your very very own mind and what you would likely say about the ones topics. Hold it lower returned. Listening with empathy lets you understand why the character allows

Candidate X, not to leap in right after "I'm going to vote—" with "Well I'm now not going to vote! I changed into so disappointed very last year..."

five. Know the benefits and drawbacks of taking notes.

It's regular to enjoy your "monkey thoughts" trying to leap earlier, in among someone else's phrases, and consider other subjects (not necessarily even truely what you want to mention subsequent). Humans count on faster than humans talk.

The neurons that make up your thoughts are aware of firing tiny electric prices round acquainted circuits at a acquainted price of velocity. Listening forces them to slow down.

For extended listening, a table or desk is a notable advantage. Those lively circuits in your brain that want to jump into motion, in maximum of the speaker's phrases, may be harnessed by the system of taking notes. If you didn't discover ways to take notes in college, it'd be precise exercising to begin doing that now. If you don't sense snug taking notes on stay conversations, attempt a web audio-e-book or documentary movie, or take a persevering with training class.

Even in cultures in which extended eye contact is ordinary, maximum human beings recognize the advantages of taking notes in a work- or college-related communique. In truth, in a "personal interview," or fitness-care-associated communication, study-taking can in reality bring together rapport.

"Writing your ebook at the same time as bringing up teenagers need to have been annoying," you will probably say, mechanically.

"Sometimes," the author might probably say, with a outstanding eye-roll.

You make a be aware.

"But don't say that," the author says. "They are even though teenagers. Let's omit the detail about sincerely one of them forgetting to tell me that the permission slips I allow him stamp my name on covered one for every week-lengthy magnificence adventure, and communicate about how useful they were as studies assistants. In fact one in every of them discovered the brand new take a look at that modified the route of factor 5..."

Note-taking can remind people to rethink hasty, stereotyped emotional reactions and recognition on their real cause.

In a few styles of remedy, "raw, unfiltered emotions" was considered greater exciting than rational mind. That thing of view stays beneficial whilst people want to break the addiction of denying that they have any socially undesirable or "awful" feelings, some element Freud might also want to have called an identity. However, empathetic litening recognizes that most people now get hold of that we've had been given ids, and want to get on with the agency of what Freud may also have called our superegos.

Sometimes some humans need to vent their unwelcome feelings to a pal or family member. More often, more human beings have reached a preference and want to cut off interest to their unwelcome emotions. Empathetic listening is achieved to what people want to talk approximately. Listening with empathy may additionally additionally moreover invite more expressions of emotion; however, it does now not disregard the real issues of people's "outer adults" as a way to explore for their "inner kids."

Note-taking does now not mechanically cut off the speaker's emotional expressions; psychotherapists historically now not handiest took notes, but sat out of the clients' line of imaginative and prescient, on the identical time as their customers poured out matters they might have determined hard to say whilst maintaining eye contact. And conditions that name for attentive, empathetic listening do now not necesssarily cognizance on emotion; their motive may be to help a affected character walk a out of doors in addition.

Nevertheless, in some private conversations, be aware-taking is seen as beside the factor. In very intimate, non-public, emotional conversations, and in a few very businesslike conversations, take a look at-taking is out of region due to the fact the listener's arms need to be unfastened—to cuddle a infant, or to carry out a tool. Mothers and toddlers don't take notes.

6. Recognize cognitive dissonance, and detach from it at the same time as that's suitable.

When someone hits six adjoining piano keys at the identical time, that kind of sound is referred to as dissonance. The notes F, A, and C form a harmonious aggregate.

The notes G, B, and D likewise appear to belong together. All six straight away make a dissonant sound. Without understanding one be aware from some different, you'd nevertheless want that dissonance to be resolved into one harmonious chord at a time.

The cognitive dissonance we sense whilst we recollect matters which can't be real on the identical time impacts our minds in something much like the manner the six adjoining notes have an impact on our ears. Did the ball land internal or outside the road? Once you've formed an opinion, you routinely grow to be a lot much less tolerant of conflicting critiques, even though they're similarly valid or maybe if the project is trivial.

Cognitive dissonance can make it difficult to pay attention information that conflict with our preconceptions, too: Even even though a few college university college students determine on dishonest to getting to know, there's physical proof that the scholar stuck dealing with another scholar's paper changed into no longer copying answers. Even despite the fact that the affected character doesn't have some of the not unusual chance elements, he has all the signs and symptoms and signs and symptoms of the disease. Even despite the fact that the youngster smells smoky, she says she left the celebration early because of the truth she didn't want a gasp on irrespective of the others had been smoking. In situations like those you experience willing to remedy the cognitive dissonance via manner of rejecting the dissonant message you're paying attention to as fake—but it's right.

One way to relieve cognitive dissonance is to undergo in mind that statements can be legitimate on numerous clearly considered one of a type degrees. Some of the topics people inform us are very near what we'd say if we have been in their feature—easy statements of truth ("It's raining") and judgments based totally on views similar to our private ("This rain's simply what the garden desired"). A few are what we'd name fake—errors, misstatements, or outright lies. Many are judgments based absolutely on the people' views (even "It's not raining" is probably proper for someone 1/2 a mile away). When a few thing said seems as even though it may't possibly be actual, empathetic listening is a useful approach for finding out why someone can also say it.

Sometimes taking note of dissonant facts presents us with new data. When experimenter Russell Targ described himself, at the the the front cowl of a ebook, as "a Blind Biker," readers predicted him to mention that he'd been a biker in advance than he have turn out to be blind. Non-readers rejected his ebook because of the fact they didn't believe it can possibly be proper. Those who went at once to check the book will keep in mind the technology Targ described as making it viable for a very nearsighted ("legally blind") man or woman to adventure a motorbike.

When babies start learning to speak, the reality that they're babies overrides all different cognitive dissonance. (Sometimes this works in competition to infants; no individual expects them to take a look at, hundreds a notable deal a good deal much less so you can speak, some aspect like "The rabid bat flew into the hall closet.") It's now not regularly useful to recall adults or maybe older children as babies. Instead it is able to be useful to use existential philosophy to their variations from us. Each mother and father studies lifestyles in such excellent strategies that it's amazing that we're capable of agree on terms to speak something the least bit.

7.   Know   strategies   to   prevent   the communication; use them mindfully.

There are literally dozens of methods to sign the quit of an lively listening consultation, further to obvious ones like "I'll pass and try this now" or "Let's give up this name now." People   don't   constantly   consciously understand that some subjects they'll be saying are serving the reason of slicing off the conversation to which they're uninterested in listening.

Perhaps the maximum not unusual way empathetic listeners by the usage of twist of fate near off audio system is with the aid of expressing a charge judgment. Listeners who aren't consciously attempting to speak "I'm bored with listening for now" may be showing assist—probable for family participants they want to inspire to percentage extra reminiscences approximately "their days" at paintings or college. "You had been right! You're this sort of dedicated employee! They have to pay you greater!" is encouraging in a few strategies, however telling the relaxation of the story isn't always what it encourages.

Ending a listening consultation is not all terrible; it could't pass on for all time. When you want the individual to inform you extra, but, whether or now not you're a scientific psychologist or a concerned decide, the most beneficial detail to say is probably "Tell me more." In non-medical conditions, versions like "And then what came about?" or "I surprise what he's going to do next" or "How did she appear to be taking the data?" can hold the tale going.

Then once more, questions that direct the narrative (specifically the "Why do you determined they did that?" or "How do you experience approximately this?" range) can also exchange the direction an excessive amount of and reduce off the story. This isn't all lousy. The speaker won't understand why someone did something or what a person is probably to do subsequent, however would in all likelihood advantage from thinking about the ones questions. Your choice is primarily based upon on your intentions.

Beyond the very basics ("Yes," "No," "Tell me extra"), a few element that's related to psychotherapy includes a exceptional integrated rate judgment that may be counterproductive in some different scenario. In some circles, even the phrase "empathy" can be risky: While psychologists now use "empathy" to speak of that primary cognizance of diverse human beings's feelings that makes verbal exchange possible, within the mid-20th century "empathy" became what scientific docs, teachers, and specifically social people have been counseled to cultivate inside the direction of clients—in amazing phrases a few component humans diagnosed as more geared up showed to people identified as an awful lot a whole lot much less prepared. If you're in psychotherapy, yourself, and located a few thing your therapist said so beneficial that you need to percentage it with every body you understand, giving due credit score rating in your therapist can help defuse the belief which you are judging one of a kind humans to be an awful lot much less succesful than you're. (It can also invite snubs: "You in no manner idea of that in advance than?")

In our first actual verbal exchange stories, there was absolute confidence that one character have end up an individual and the opportunity have become a toddler. This truth now and again obscures our reminiscence of the quantity to which, in empathetic listening, the person mirrors the child. Parents set aside stereotyped mind ("Rain is uninteresting; the a good deal much less we be conscious it, the better") and percent the kid's perception ("Rain is exciting; dust is interesting; a shoe full of water is thrilling"), improved through the child's pleasure in reading to talk. Adults "come to be childlike," and revel in it.

When we take note of adults with empathy, we also can become student-like, instructor-like, supervisor-like, arthritic-stroke-survivor-like, grumpy-consumer-like, and so forth—and experience it. Stepping back, even into our agreed-upon roles, breaks a bond and ought to be finished mindfully.

Chapter 3: Learning to Listen at Work

When you start listening with empathy in the administrative center, you could come across some administrative center-specific communique conditions and controversies. No e-book may additionally need to anticipate all the opportunities. Here are a few tips on 3 not unusual place of business communique problems.

What is a sensory mode desire, and does it rely wide variety?

Since approximately 1970, humans analyzing the psychology of business enterprise and training have debated the idea that every parents continuously relies on truly one in every of 3 primary sensory channels—sight, taking note of, or touch—for wondering and gaining knowledge of. People who intuitively experience that this idea is actual and vital, logically, are people whose sensory mode options are specifically strong (and/or particular from what others count on). People who doubt that it's actual or that it's crucial might be human beings whose options are lots less robust.

Despite current neurological development, it stays tough to quantify the quantity to which normal mind techniques involve one sensory channel or each different. Individuals range. There is some basis for the assertion that the entire idea of sensory options is "pseudoscience." Nevertheless, there also are teachers, managers, salesmen, psychologists, and authors who've constructed a success careers on the use of it, so it's sincerely definitely worth considering what's been found approximately this mental precept within the final fifty years.

The cliché in truth everybody observed out within the Nineteen Eighties have turn out to be that common male students are visible thinkers, common woman college students are tactile thinkers, and "talented" college students are auditory thinkers. As a stereotype this end up reasonably correct, and it's easy to provide an explanation for.

The recognition on reading and writing, within the conventional university machine, does selectively need auditory rookies. I.Q. Exams generally generally tend to yield excessive ratings for auditory novices and low scores for tactile beginners. This is one of the strategies wherein I.Q. Checks because it must be are awaiting fulfillment in conventional school rooms however emerge as much less correct for predicting achievement in adults' careers.

But in truth, for masses humans, sensory mode selections don't seem like very robust or consistent. While Suzette Haden Elgin modified into capable of assist a few humans whose strong desire for tactile studying and wondering created difficulties for them, Elgin identified herself first as a seen thinker and then as a tactile philosopher (based totally totally mostly on early exams) before spotting herself as an auditory fact seeker. That sort of confusion have become not unusual in her goal marketplace, every. That aim market protected the form of phrase-nerds who quibbled: "Well...Elgin's nonfiction books about language are about as 'auditory' because it's feasible for books to be, whether or no longer or now not she's a visible philosopher inside the rest of her lifestyles or not...I appreciate her books, this is 'auditory,' but then I additionally paintings as a rub down therapist, that is 'tactile,' to pay the payments while I struggle for success as a painter!" When tests of sensory mode picks were set up to yield percent scores, pretty some humans had scores like 32-35-33.

A refinement of the easy idea that served Dawna Markova nicely indicates that every folks has a most conscious, least aware, and "subconscious" mode choice. Elgin, for instance, have become tremendous noted for writing books about language; throughout her career her entire-time jobs as typist, creator, trainer, hassle linguist, and psycholinguist fell into the "auditory, verbal" category, however she moreover loved some success as a seen artist, and used gardening for rest and meditation. For many human beings whose capabilities and interests showed a 32-35-33 stability amongst sensory modes, there has been a comparable stability the severa sensory modes that dominated their primary careers, a sideline or interest that might have emerge as a 2d career, and subjects they "did genuinely to lighten up."

Another refinement that has labored for optimum instructors who've been able to try it have become "The extra sensory channels it's viable to engage in mastering some thing, the higher." In a conventional secondary or tertiary schoolroom, the remarkable college students each assist themselves studies extra efficiently, and guarantee academics that the students are listening, thru "listening" with their eyes and hands in addition to their ears.

The college college students watch the lecturer's face (and gestures and posture) for aditional statistics, and additionally they take notes on the lecture. This method also works in profits.

Still, studies of sensory desire are a protracted manner from being a settled technology. For many humans, involuntary eye actions suggest which sensory channel has their hobby from 2nd to second, however it's no longer usually viable to discover a everyday sample, or to rely upon it for correct statistics. Some humans seem to fasten into quality one channel underneath pressure; many do not. Perhaps because of the truth psychotherapists who labored with Neuro-Linguistic Programming techniques consciously relied on sensory mode terms to construct rapport, people who make an effort to do that in business enterprise on occasion decided a backfire impact.

A potential client who's familiar with NLP principle will apprehend a non-tactile thinker's try to encompass greater tactile terms in communication, and can resent or resist them, possibly questioning "Just due to the truth I use a few tactile terms, don't assume you could write me off as a person who best ever thinks in touch mode!"

Furthermore, income resistance may be slightly reduced, however it's nevertheless there, whilst sellers and possibilities are the use of the equal sensory modes.

"It appears particular right proper right here, now, but how will that color react to three years of sunlight hours and weather?"

"It sounds super, however will that sound actually be outstanding enough to justify that charge? For how prolonged?"

"It feels satisfactory, however how prolonged will it art work 'like new'? How masses placed on and tear can it take?"

There is not any replacement for appropriate great and truthful prices...No rely a shop clerk's use of sensory modes.

For most people, there also can or won't be a easy advantage in matching sensory modes whilst it's feasible to transport all of the manner—supply tactile thinkers samples to touch, show visible thinkers images, in location of relying on words. The benefit is a good deal lots less smooth at the same time as all you're capable of do is match terms. Saying "I see what you imply" received't compensate if your pix don't illustrate what the consumer way; asking "Does this revel in proper?" won't trade the reality if your product feels all incorrect.

However, if paying attention to a person shows that this character does depend closely on visible or tactile questioning, deciding on phrases that healthful that sensory mode can reduce the stress and enhance the person's capacity to pay attention to your facet of the problem. Better yet, look for techniques to offer statistics nonverbally. For visible thinkers a amazing map or graph certainly is without a doubt well worth one thousand words; a video can be even better. For tactile thinkers a version or sample is worth 1000 pics.

Online, this precept works the other way too: some humans want to be reminded that, for auditory thinkers (and for maximum website online traffic to a business company internet internet site), an audiovisual show is useless display screen clutter that their laptop has in all likelihood been programmed no longer even to open. If you want to pick amongst undeniable text and a video, textual content might be extra accessible to extra site visitors.

There are famous pc accessories that might translate text into distinct languages, read it aloud, or maybe encode it as Braille, however there's no way for people traveling your net website online from a public location to decode a message that's been located on-line as a video.

What are the 16 man or woman sorts, and what shape of does that depend range?

The ebook Type Talk identifies sixteen character sorts based totally on in which humans fall most of the extremes of 4 measurable inclinations: introvert or extrovert, sensing or instinct, wondering or feeling, and judging or perceiving. For comfort each kind is summarized thru 4 letters: ISTJ, ENFP, or some wonderful aggregate.

As a era, psychology have become constrained to a "philosophical degree" of generalization based totally on semi-subjective observations for a long term. Psychologists who attempting to find recognition as "real" scientists sometimes rush to push aside what clinical, educational, and enterprise psychologists have observed out because it's not primarily based on neurological studies of the brain. Like maximum person theories, the Myers-Briggs personality models wholesome many humans very well, though not all of us. (There are humans whose self-test rankings fall in the center of every of the four continuums.)

People can and do consciously select out to behave contrary to their herbal options. This is mainly possibly to take area in conditions in which people's herbal options have been disparaged by means of manner of the encompassing subculture as "inclined," "neurotic," "unscientific," "unfeminine," or "immature." Kroeger referred to at some duration the hostility determined inside the Nineteen Seventies while North American women expressed "unfeminine" NTJ tendencies.

Other writers have documented the hostility Freud's enthusiasts confirmed inside the path of introverts throughout Europe and North America. This also can had been a kind of backlash. Into the Renaissance, extrovert behavior have been diagnosed as an terrible greater of "sanguine humours," for which the same vintage treatment modified into bloodletting: "Sanguine women and men are...Even presumptuous, requiring a common use of phlebotomy."

Humans adjust their conduct to match their environments. While neurological studies have not begun to affirm physical dispositions that shape everlasting alternatives for the other man or woman characteristics, we now realise that as a minimum wholesome, everlasting physical traits help to supply introvert personalities. Freud, running with those who had already developed number one intellectual infection, seemed capable of recognize a choice to artwork by myself satisfactory as a transient a part of the prodrome to a psychotic breakdown.

That phenomenon does exist...But so do wholesome introverts who clearly increase greater entire neurological "wiring" than extroverts do, understand subjects in more element, and assume matters through in extra depth. As introverts recognize their hereditary traits as benefits (certainly correlated with longer energetic lives), a brand new backlash may also already be starting at some colleges, wherein "outgoing" youngsters are all over again being referred for clinical remedy.

Many companies have actively discriminated closer to introverts in the beyond. Some however do. And courtroom cases in opposition to corporations wherein, for instance, individuals who don't encourage chatter from pushy earnings frame of people have been burdened with overtly unfavourable chatter, are probable beneath manner somewhere on the time of writing. While introverts through manner of way of definition don't want to have hobby called to them in offices, it might likely be an wonderful concept for business owners and personnel to begin enhancing their introvert verbal exchange talents now. Those skills would possibly encompass things like studying to lower returned away gracefully while clients don't encourage chatter, lowering glare, clutter, and noise, and selecting to lessen marketing fees and skip the financial financial savings directly to clients, in addition to schooling personnel to pay interest with empathy.

Generally, whether or not or now not you find out that either the Myers-Briggs character training, the "classical four temperaments," or every other simplified model of character kinds suits the people you apprehend excellent, an incredible business business employer approach is to apprehend that the differences exist. Then, without obsessively seeking to classify all and sundry you meet inside the administrative center, you can use empathetic taking note of grow to be aware about and art work with the personality trends the person offers to you on any given day.

People who say such things as "How clinical is that this version?" are presently engaged in wondering and judging. They're seeking out concrete, rational solutions in place of intuitive, philosophical ones. If you don't have a solution complete of facts and facts to offer them, tell them you'll get returned to them with one, then look up the data and p.C. As many numbers into your answer as feasible.

People who say such things as "How can we have interaction empathy and compassion for...?" are currently engaged in perceiving and feeling. They're seeking out answers that appeal to their and their intention marketplace's feelings (on the equal time as status up to fact finding out). For them, "Last 12 months our business enterprise helped 423 human beings like Lee," with a picture of someone who appears to had been in need of help, might be a higher lead-in than "Last 12 months our agency raised $3500 for..."

Were humans taught to make statements and ask questions right away, or drop and look earlier to diffused suggestions?

The difference amongst "Ask cultures" and "Hint cultures" is not simply correlated with any ethnic or socioeconomic divisions, even though a few humans have notion it emerge as. It's a discovered behavior pattern. Some humans recall, especially, that soliciting for things not directly is looking greater "well" than asking straight away, on the identical time as others bypass so far as to assert that "Hinting is evil."

In a pluralistic society, it's smooth to assist the argument—which a few psychotherapists have endorsed—that we have to all artwork to dispose of some thing inclinations we may additionally additionally have shaped to search for recommendations in desire to asking direct questions. Hints are with out difficulty misinterpret, and those who huff that a person "shouldn't want to ask that" in reality appear to be arrogant and judgmental.

For some people, "Ask cultures" dominate the administrative center no matter the reality that "Hint way of lifestyles" behavior is nice at home. Women business enterprise owners of a certain age are specially probably to certainly receive as genuine with in bold, direct, forthright behavior in enterprise meetings, on the equal time as feeling that their "desire to be requested" for social invites proves that they're however "feminine."

Nevertheless, we nevertheless meet folks who enjoy that subtle recommendations are extra tactful than direct requests. As prolonged as they are capable to break out with their sidelong glances and murmurs,

"Don't you trust you studied it's cold in right here?", they probable will hold to experience that this conduct is "nicer" than sincerely saying "I'm feeling cold." As prolonged as some of the ones humans are without a doubt awesome, type, and stressful souls, others will possibly believe them.

If you have got were given been added up in a "Hint lifestyle," looking to end up greater cushty with "Ask way of life" might be a brilliant concept. (After all, the diffused tips you've placed out to use are possibly to be all wrong for every other "Hint lifestyle.") However, listening with empathy can assist humans understand even as human beings from high-quality "Hint cultures" are seeking to drop diffused hints, as a minimum, if no longer to guess what the ones recommendations may mean.

Chapter 4: Learning to Listen in a Close Relationship

Since we find out techniques to speak with the aid of manner of way of listening with our complete hobby, if now not with person-kind empathy, in a near relationship, it appears to go together with out saying that attentive, empathetic listening belongs in the distinct close relationships we form later in existence. Home is the place to use our top notch listening abilities.

Since circle of relatives relationships generally comprise humans of various some time and sexes, this phase may be the top notch location to consider communication problems particularly related to age and intercourse.

Sex: Gender stereotypes and individuals

In the film When Harry Met Sally, Meg Ryan ("Sally") showed one of the most not unusual methods higher halves lie to their husbands— pretending to experience intercourse as loads because the husbands do, even as in fact they're not even fascinated, truly to get to sleep (or to art work) faster. Richard Cohen, writing in The Washington Post Magazine, indignantly retorted that husbands are similarly misleading, manipulative, and proficient for acting: in step with Cohen maximum if now not all husbands "fake listening."

People who really do "faux listening" are the ones most probably to consider that all guys and all women, or as a minimum those who are "certainly" masculine or woman, conform to as a minimum one norm—for some thing, sincerely, beyond having physical sex traits.

Men are taller, on not unusual, than girls are. Some women are taller than some guys are.

Women take extra hobby in toddlers and younger kids, on common, than men do. Some guys are more committed to their children than a few girls are.

Men are much more likely to enjoy and precise anger, on common, than ladies are. (This tendency is associated with guys's

73

tendency to increase cardiovascular sickness and die in advance than ladies do.) Some girls are more violent than a few men are.

It may be real that, as C.S. Lewis had a clever fictional person inform a extra younger individual, "no person ought to sincerely concentrate to all of the things we say." It's additionally real that, as Elizabeth Zimmermann found of her very personal marriage, after years together human beings have informed every special most of what they at the begin preferred to mention and can enjoy being quiet collectively.

Many, if no longer maximum, marriages are among a talker and a listener.

Either the spouse or the husband can be the talker; each may be the listener. While famous subculture shows that "talks an excessive amount of" has been part of a gender stereotype for every sexes, counting on the time and area, it can be more beneficial to go through in thoughts the tendency to talk more than pay interest relative to cardiovascular health in place of gender. People of every sexes may also moreover moreover make bigger their healthy lifestyles expectancy by means of the usage of analyzing to pay interest.

It's but actual that, if the aim is quiet intimacy at domestic, the shortest manner to obtain that intention is to pay hobby attentively to every word (or as many as viable of the phrases) your family say. Knowing that what they've said has been heard relieves the compulsion a few humans feel to mention things time and again. Eventually higher halves and husbands (and dad and mom and their grownup youngsters) can attain a problem in which they've advised each unique who they may be and revel in a need to speak first-rate approximately what's new from every day.

Meanwhile, the early years of marriage are the herbal place for "placing on (each distinct's) each word," with whole hobby, prolonged eye contact, and all that certainly follows. Attentive listening is maximum of the maximum erotic topics couples can do.

Age: Generations, some time, tiers

While youngsters become snug with the "Run along, I'm busy" degree of hobby at a very early age, communication among parents and youngsters stays critical as children are developing up. As cited, mother and father who pay interest with empathy, not rushing in to trouble orders before youngsters have a danger to finish their mind, are those in all likelihood to have children who enlist their help with community issues like drug hobby in choice to being sucked into the troubles.

Listening to children with empathy does not mean being "permissive." In reality it could mean spotting whilst youngsters want a bit of parental authority.

"Olivia invited me to spend spring ruin collectively along with her family," eighteen-yr-antique Emily might also say.

"Tell me greater."

"Well, her own family live in Cleveland...She stated they're all heavy drinkers, but her sister Amber's the first-rate one who's really in Alcoholics Anonymous...Olivia's the fine who had a infant even as she have end up fourteen, and her mom's been rearing it. I count on she'll need to spend most of the time checking in collectively along with her toddler."

"So, you're thinking you'd be spending greater time gaining knowledge of the relaxation of her family?"

"Yes, and he or she's in no way made them sound as though I'd like them."

"Who's the father of Olivia's infant? Is there a threat that he'll be on the scene?"

"Yes...Truly he's the brother-in-regulation who's dwelling in conjunction with her sister in her mother and father' basement."

At this issue empathetic listening will likely spark off Emily's mom to mention, "I don't anticipate it's a terrific idea if you want to spend every week underneath the identical roof with a extra younger guy who molested his partner's fourteen-three hundred and sixty five days-antique sister. What did you tell Olivia?"

Empathetic listening is also in all likelihood to have made it feasible for Emily to mention, "I knowledgeable her I'd talk to you about it first," and for Emily's mother to mention, "Let me speak this together collectively along with your father," right away, and suggest, day after today, "Why don't you inform Olivia you're going with us to (everywhere)?"

Of path there's moreover a possibility that Emily may additionally rebellion. "Well she's my pal and I expect I must be along side her for moral help, mainly because of the reality her brother-in-law..." Empathetic listening received't eliminate disagreements amongst circle of relatives people; but it is able to help them remedy conflicts without anger. Emily's probable dodged some unwelcome advances by manner of now, and he or she or he clearly may additionally have worked out a possible strategy to help Olivia keep away from being abused all once more. If blessed with dad and mom who pay interest with empathy, she may additionally also be able to give an explanation for this approach inside the kind of manner that they might consider it.

Teenagers grow up, and branch out far from the antique family tree, anyhow. Likewise, dad and mom develop antique. Listening with empathy is as essential in speakme with growing older dad and mom as it is in speaking with teenaged youngsters.

In reality, as has frequently been determined, stressful for growing older parents has an awful lot in not unusual with stressful for growing children. The identical fiddly little info need to be remembered; the same boring little chores can also want to be supervised; the identical acquainted excuses and sneaky verbal assaults may be heard. The hard aspect may be remembering that getting older dad and mom aren't kids. They understand what they need, and are fully capable of making selections for themselves, even though they depend on us to place into impact the ones selections at the same time as they will be ill.

There is an unfortunate tendency for a few younger people to assume that, every time older humans stop trying to look younger, they're senile. In fact most human beings with snow-white hair, even if further they have pneumonia and don't enjoy like speakme, recognize what's taking place spherical them higher than these more youthful human beings do. Most human beings in no way enlarge Alzheimer's Disease. Many folks who do increase great disabling conditions in vintage age simply surrender dwelling when they understand that humans round them anticipate they have got Alzheimer's Disease. For a person who simply has Parkinson's Disease, or a few specific circumstance that impacts the potential to speak, there's no "satisfaction" within the consciousness that specific humans accept as true with that "moments of delight" are all they have got left. Being relegated to "moments of pride" may be overwhelmingly depressing; it's a reason of suicide.

On the opposite hand, for a person who honestly has Alzheimer's Disease (and remains conscious sufficient to recognize that analysis), seeking to take into account matters might also additionally produce useless distress that aggravates and hastens the sickness.

People can lose the functionality to speak, preserve new memories, do not forget vintage ones on name for, apprehend faces, maintain in mind how they have been given into the medical institution—quick—and then get higher all the ones abilties, because of any quantity of factors, at any age. Genuine dementia is more likely to be a quick impact of fever, medicinal drugs, and chemical imbalances than of Alzheimer's Disease.

So, if we assume that elderly human beings have Alzheimer's Disease and take delivery of "developing moments of satisfaction" after they're nevertheless capable of apprehend that we "lied to" them, we're doing them harm; if we count on that they don't have Alzheimer's Disease and are probably to get higher the entire use in their brains, any day, once they do have Alzheimer's Disease, we're doing them damage. How is it feasible to recognize how to speak to any antique person who appears stressed in any way? As Jolene Brackey determined in Creating Moments of Joy, "Listening is magical."

Old age is not for wimps, in any case. Empathetic listening lets in a extraordinary deal.

Empathetic listening is in truth the exceptional way exceptional "senile" behaviors may be understood...Even even though, whilst understood, they make perfect feel.

An 85-year-antique affected man or woman who had had a few slight strokes recovered an lousy lot of his out of vicinity capability to walk, speak, preserve in thoughts, and revel in favored ingredients after it have emerge as feasible to lessen his blood stress medicine. He preferred sitting outdoors and searching his accomplice and kids cultivate the garden. He cherished sniffing and tasting the sparkling produce even because it have come to be picked, or maybe helped shell peas. Yet, even as food had been on the desk, he took one well mannered little chunk of the whole lot, took a long term to swallow it and pronounce it accurate, and then set about methodically mashing the whole lot together proper proper right into a disgusting mess at the plate.

To be rude? To show what he in reality idea of his loved ones' cooking? One of his own family attempted dumping the whole lot into the blender. The affected character ate extra of every meal even as it modified into warmth that way. After a few strokes, the delight of tasting every separate taste had turn out to be secondary to the need to make the entirety as easy as possible to swallow; the affected person now not loved perfect manipulate of his private chewing and swallowing.

In this situation, it have become the affected individual's nonverbal behavior that had to be "listened to" with empathy. This is often actual for humans with any shape of chronic incapacity, at the side of, however now not limited to, any form of thoughts or nerve damage.

"Autistic" patients are a modern elegance of own family folks who want attentive listening, not only to any phrases they will use, but to their nonverbal conduct.

The incidence of diagnoses of autism has skyrocketed in the previous few years. One cause for this is virtually that the jogging analysis of autism has modified. In the early 20th century "autistic behavior" become a technical term from time to time used to explain subjects people did really for his or her private amusement or gratification, with out a connection with others, like buzzing or nail-biting. Then "autism" have become a extra tactful analysis for the kind of thoughts damage that renders communication with others now not feasible, for which the formal term was once idiocy. Then, across the turn of the century, investment for research and rehabilitative art work with "autistic children" generated enough hobby in a specific neurological ailment ("ballooning mind") related to autism that the interest spilled over. Today, within the United States, the label of "autism" is every so often applied to—and embraced via—more youthful those who, a generation earlier, may want to have insisted that what they've got is cerebral palsy, a totally splendid element.

Another cause is that the occurrence of unmistakable mind damage has elevated. We've end up more acquainted with seeing kids whose eyes don't attention in colleges than we changed into; however, greater youngsters are attaining college age with eyes that don't interest.

The announcing became, "If communique is feasible, the child doesn't have autism." This is now not ordinary. Because the modern-day operating definition of autism is so large as to be useless for the cause of meticulous studies, the present day pronouncing is, "If you've seen one affected man or woman with autism, you've seen one affected individual with autism." Generalizations approximately the effects of ballooning brains are possible. Generalizations approximately the outcomes of a term that could consist of any sort of eternal damage, not on time development, or transient malfunction of any a part of the mind, aren't feasible.

Charismatic public figures from Temple Grandin to Greta Thunberg, on the same time as succeeding as complete-time professional communicators, in reality have brains burdened out in a exceptional way from different human beings and demand that their difference be called a form of autism. Who taught those people to talk any language (some of them communicate numerous languages), and the way? The solution to that is that the folks who taught them to speak listened to them with empathy. Temple Grandin can tell us a way to speak together together with her; her insights can also moreover or won't provide any useful thoughts for speaking along aspect your autistic nephew. You should start at the begin, listening empathetically to what that infant can and cannot say in phrases.

Actually, listening with empathy is what's made it feasible for plenty people with cerebral palsy, paralysis, lack of sight or taking note of, or particular disabilities to speak too.

Chapter 5: Learning to Listen to Retain Information

Retaining statistics is most possibly to be the purpose of listening in a schoolroom. Since maximum oldsters pass to school earlier than we do jobs and begin families, why is that this section located after the sections on listening in workplaces and families? Right: this quick phase is particularly for humans returning to high school as adults.

When schools get hold of extra investment and special types of assist for any try and combine more human beings with particular sorts of disabilities into mainstream schooling, always the whole thing starts offevolved to appear to be a disability to everybody who have to use more funding.

"We supported efforts to steady instructional possibilities for individuals who have been 'legally blind,' like Hillary Clinton, who changed into earning top grades at a top university at the identical time as she end up not often succesful to walk round without her eyeglasses," an American activist recalled with chagrin. "Then we went back to instructions and heard 23-twelve months-olds sprezzing on about whether or not or not they deserved extra credit score because of the truth 17-12 months-olds' more younger eyes might be able to test quicker, for pity's sake. If you're 25 or maybe 50 years vintage, and the gain of your extra famous expertise does no longer absolutely offset any gain a 17-12 months-antique receives from being able to read quicker, then I'd must wonder what benefit you could get from any type of training."

Most folks who are 25 or 50 years vintage can of path get a few benefit from most of the educational opportunities which can be to be had to us. (Among exclusive topics, they may help protect our brains from the growing vintage system.) "Sprezzing," a slang phrase lengthy-hooked up from the musical time period sprezzatura (for "performing with feeling"), want to not be crucial. All we're being asked to do is examine.

Of course we've slept even as you recollect that we ultimate filled in records for a massive test. Not only that, however the content fabric of the big take a look at is likely to have changed. Science and records publications have changed to consist of new chapters in statistics. Works of literature haven't changed, however the listing of which matches are currently considered essential has. Even mathematics publications have modified, in recognition and in coaching technique: these days, because the capability to apply computer systems is so crucial to employers and mathematics is naturally perfect to on line getting to know, some arithmetic guides can be taught almost in reality on-line.

How do older college students address the call for that we rearrange the contents of our intellectual garage files, which have served us pretty well, outside the have a examine room, for the past ten or twenty or fifty years? We do the identical subjects extra younger college college students want to do to fill their highbrow storage documents for the number one time. We use the identical look at capabilities they do. Overall the quantity of highbrow try involved in updating what we comprehend at age fifty might be tons a good deal less than the amount worried in getting to know it for the first time at fifeen. It's that pervasive sense that we've got "no time to kill" that makes us experience so busy, as if the need to have a study have been a greater intellectual burden than it became.

If you sense especially challenged thru the concept of going again to school or taking a class, a very helpful on line micro-course in "have a have a take a look at talents" is on line, free of rate, at Alison.Com. Lists of "take a look at skills" may be broken proper down to itemize dozens of numerous strategies to reading, but there's big settlement about the essential importance of three meta-competencies for buying the most out of any path of look at:

1. Stay out of problem—scientific, jail, emotional, and a few special type. Even parking tickets or misplaced library books are needless distractions.

2. Go to each elegance assembly and do each hobby the instructor assigns or recommends that will help you absorb information from ordinary. Don't attempt to cram everything into the week, or day, earlier than the very last exam. Plan on at the least an hour of studying to put together for a lecture or talk, and an hour of evaluation to make certain you get the benefit of the lecture or communicate. (As a well-known rule, the more prestigious the college and/or path is considered to be, the faster the magnificence will circulate and the greater prep and evaluation time you'll need.)

three. Listen to the teacher (and, if discussions and seminars are part of the path, your classmates). The more material is posted on-line, the greater vital it will become to cite what you found out or did in elegance in your final paper. Teachers increasingly rely upon this proof that the paper is your private actual art work. Listen carefully throughout every elegance meeting. Choose your references properly.

The Internet gives nearly endless strategies to extend our running memory. While it's nonetheless essential to apprehend a way to location sentences together and calculate numbers with out get proper of access to to any virtual tool, reasonably-priced calculators and "smart phones" permit us to look some factor up, almost everywhere, at nearly any time. The risk is that relying on those memory aids may additionally moreover make it easy to miss subjects we need to maintain in thoughts: Because your sister's mobile telephone variety is programmed into your mobile phone, wherein it pops up on the contact of 1 button that corresponds to her initial, you don't problem to memorize her cellular phone range, and want to dig thru a drawer entire of scraps of paper to find out it on the same time as you want to software program it into your new cell mobile phone.

There's no reason why the generation that invented the Internet ought to have any specific hassle in reading to apply it. In fact, if older human beings aren't required to take "recertification" or "continuing schooling" guides for his or her jobs, it might be a good idea to take some online publications except...To keep our brains energetic.

Though online conversation may additionally moreover seem to put off "the human touch," once we end up acquainted with the Internet, it's genuinely every other way to pay hobby.

Chapter 6: Understanding the Elements of Communication

How Do We Communicate?

To outline, forecast, and understand the behaviors and occurrences that make-up verbal exchange, severa theories have been advocate. We are frequently much a lot much less worried with idea with regards to organization verbal exchange than we're with making sure that our messages get the supposed consequences. However, it might be useful to recognize what conversation is and the way it features to get consequences.

Communication Definition

Latin's talk root, because of this that to percentage or make commonplace, is the supply of the English time period "communique." The gadget of comprehending and changing which means is referred to as conversation.

The connection that incorporates participant touch is at the coronary coronary heart of our studies into verbal exchange. With its popularity at the system for efficaciously facts and sharing some other character's point of view, which we're going to discover in-depth throughout this artwork, this definition is helpful to us.

The manner is the definition's first important term. Because it changes, a method is a dynamic interest that is hard to give an explanation for. Assume you're by myself on your kitchen, thinking of some element. You in quick converse with the person who enters the kitchen (permit's fake it's miles your mum). What's one of a kind now? Imagine that similarly on your mother, there can be now a stranger you have got by no means met, and they will be attentively being attentive to everything you're pronouncing, almost as if you had been handing over a speech. What's high-quality now? You should alter your angle, and you may pay closer interest to what you are saying. You might also moreover moreover want to rethink what you are saying in slight of your mother's and the stranger's feedback or reactions, who're basically your target marketplace. All of those elements, together with a incredible variety more, have an impact on how we talk while we've got were given interplay.

"To understand is to recognize, to interpret, and to apply our observation and interpretation to what we already recognize," states the second one important time period. What photograph includes thoughts even as a friend tells you a story approximately falling off a motorbike? Your companion now gestures toward the window, in which you may see a motorcycle at the ground. Understanding the phrases and the mind or topics they allude to is critical to powerful communique.

Sharing is the following word. Sharing refers to acting with one or extra other humans. You can collaborate on an hobby, inclusive of at the same time as you put together a file together, or you may every use and take advantage of a resource, like even as you and your colleagues break up a pizza. When you speak your thoughts, emotions, thoughts, or insights to others, you're sharing. You may communicate with your self while you revel in "Aha!" moments whilst some issue ultimately makes experience, at the same time as mind spring to thoughts, while you mirror at the way you enjoy about a few thing, or at the same time as you resolve a problem. This approach is referred to as intrapersonal verbal exchange.

Finally, which means that is what we talk approximately. The term "motorcycle" may speak to a motorbike as well as a bicycle. We can determine the phrase's common which means that and understand the message thru searching at the context wherein it's miles used and with the aid of asking questions.

The Eight Crucial Elements of Communication

We may moreover divide the communique machine into a sequence of 8 vital factors to realize it better:

Source

Message

Channel

Receiver

Feedback

Environment

Context

Interference

These eight factors all play a important feature in the complete manner. Let's take a look at every one in turn.

Source

The message is created, imagined, and sent via the deliver. The speaker is the supply on the equal time as speaking within the front of an target marketplace. By offering the goal marketplace with easy records, he or she communicates the message. The speaker may moreover make a announcement with their body language, tone of voice, and attire. Before talking, the speaker need to decide what to say and the manner to specific it.

Encoding the message includes selecting the excellent terms or a particular arrangement to talk the message's supposed that means within the 2d segment. Presenting or sending the information to the intention marketplace or recipient is the 0.33 phase. Finally, the supply determines if the message end up understood through the goal marketplace via watching their response and then clarifies or gives evidence in reaction.

Message

The stimulus or that means that the supply creates for the target audience or recipient is called the message. (2005) McLean Your message may additionally moreover appear to be confined to the terms you select to unique your due to this as you prepare to deliver a speech or write a record. But it's far in reality the start. Grammar and structure assist to put together the terms. You can decide to maintain your most important argument till very last. The way you're saying it—in a speech, together with your tone of voice, your frame language, and your appearance—in addition to the manner you write it—collectively with your grammar, writing fashion, and the headers and formatting you select out—moreover make a contribution to the message. Additionally, the location or context in which you supply your message similarly to any ancient beyond noise that may make it difficult to pay hobby or see it is able to be part of the message.

Consider that you are talking to a huge institution of income representatives and which you are conscious that the World Series is being performed this night time. You may need to determine to begin via manner of way of pronouncing, "I recognize there can be an crucial recreation this night," notwithstanding the fact that your audience ought to in all likelihood find out it tough to loosen up.

By orally affirming some thing that almost all of your audience is aware about and inquisitive about, you will be able to seize and keep their hobby.

Channel

"The channel is the route taken by means of the use of a message or messages as they're sent from supply to recipient." Think of your tv for instance. How many tv channels do you've got? Even in a digital environment, the cable or signal that is composed of every channel's message to your home takes up some place.

A visible sign which you see and an auditory sign that you pay interest are jumbled collectively television.

They artwork collectively to speak the message to the target audience or recipient. Your tv's amount must be reduced. Can you still make experience of what is taking location? Many times you may for the cause that part of the content material cloth of the act is communicated via body language. Increase the amount now, but appearance some distance from the tv so you can't see it. The language remains audible, and the plot remains clean.

In a comparable vein, you operate a channel at the same time as you talk or write to supply your message. Face-to-face conversation, speeches, cellular telephone calls and voice mail, radio, public address systems, and voice-over-Internet protocol are examples of spoken channels (VoIP). Letters, memos, purchase orders, invoices, newspaper and mag articles, blogs, emails, texts, tweets, and distinct written styles of communique are examples of written channels.

Receiver

Receiving the verbal exchange from the source, the receiver analyzes and interprets it in strategies that the supply won't have meant. Consider a soccer institution receiver to have a better understanding of this element. A receiver must see the football (or message) being thrown with the useful resource of the quarterback to choose out in which to capture it. The quarterback might also moreover want the receiver to "capture" his message in a pleasing way, however the receiver may additionally furthermore interpret sports in another manner and fail to realise the quarterback's intended which means that.

You may additionally additionally gather a message as a receiver via listening, seeing, touching, smelling, and/or tasting. Long earlier than you hit the stage or talk, your audience is "sizing you up," truely as you could do. Your listeners' nonverbal cues assist you to determine the way to alter your starting. You may assume what you will look for if you were them with the resource of setting yourself in their shoes.

You can examine the interplay amongst deliver and receiver in a corporate communication putting, hundreds as a quarterback predicts wherein the receiver can be to location the ball efficiently. The simultaneous occurrence of all of these sports suggests how and why verbal exchange is typically evolving.

Feedback

Whether on reason or by way of coincidence, you are imparting feedback whilst you react to the deliver. The messages that the recipient transmits decrease lower back to the source make up remarks. Whether they may be vocal or nonverbal, all of these remarks indicators provide the conversation's originator perception into how efficaciously (or how badly) the message changed into acquired.

Feedback moreover offers the audience or receiver the threat to specific their agreement or war of phrases with the supply or to suggest approaches wherein the deliver also can make the message greater engaging. The accuracy of conversation rises together with the amount of remarks.

Consider being a profits supervisor and becoming a member of a conference name with 4 income representatives. As the dealer, you need to direct the salespeople to apply the World Series season as an opportunity to clinch offers on baseball-related sporting items. You deliver your message, however your target market does now not respond. Although you'll recollect that they understood and agreed with you, you is probably dissatisfied to research that most effective a small form of purchases had been made in some time inside the month. If you requested for feedback after your message ("Does this make feel? Do any of you have were given any questions? "), you could have the hazard to complex in your component and examine if any of the profits representatives idea your solution may want to now not fly with their customers.

Environment

"The environment is the physical and mental putting in which you transmit and acquire signs and symptoms." The fixtures in the room, along with the tables, chairs, lights, and sound device, is probably taken into consideration part of the environment. The setting is exemplified thru the room itself. A talk can be open and compassionate or more formal, formal, and expert depending on the surroundings, which may embody factors like a right attire. When people are physical near to every different, they may be greater inclined to have interaction in an intimate speak than even as they're capable of excellent see each different in the course of the room. They may additionally textual content every considered one of a kind in the sort of scenario, that's a non-public shape of touch. The environment has an impact on whether or no longer or not or now not a person texts. Your surroundings ought to have an impact on and a factor to play on your voice as a speaker. It's a wonderful idea to go to the venue earlier than the presentation day to get a feel for the distance.

Context

The backdrop, state of affairs, and expectations of the events engaged are all part of the communication interplay's context. Business suits are an instance of environmental signs that might have an effect on participant expectations for language and behavior in a expert communication scenario.

A presentation or debate isn't always a standalone prevalence.

You got here from somewhere even as to procure to beauty. Both the person who sat next to you and the trainer felt the same way. The participants' contextual expectancies for communique will decide how formal or informal the scenario is. The man or woman sitting subsequent to you'll be used to casual verbal exchange with professors, but this particular professor is probably acquainted with vocal and nonverbal symptoms of deference in a school room placing.

Your classmate's question, "Hey Teacher, are we able to have homework in recent times?" may additionally strike you as unpleasant and rude due to the fact you are used to extra formal encounters with instructors. You may additionally furthermore tell how the teacher feels approximately the interplay—along with the phrase options and the manner they have been said—by way of manner of manner of staring at their nonverbal cues.

People's expectations approximately every one of a kind are what context is all about, and we frequently shape these assumptions based on contextual clues. Weddings and quinceaneras are examples of formal activities. There are appropriate times for silent social greetings, for the bride to head down the aisle in silence, and for the father to bop along together with his daughter as she turns into a lady inside the eyes of her society.

There can be moments of boisterous dancing and birthday party in every party. You can be requested to make a toast, and the occasions of the wedding or quinceanera will affect the manner you painting your self whilst to speak, and the way a success you're.

Who talks first in a commercial commercial enterprise corporation putting? That most probably has some trouble to do with the position and feature that every member plays outdoor of the assembly. Particularly at the equal time as talking throughout cultures, context is crucial.

Interference

Noise, frequently called interference, may also originate from any supply. Anything that prevents or alters the message's intended meaning in keeping with the deliver is taken into consideration interference. For example, if you commuted with the useful resource of car to work or faculty, noise have become probably all round you. Your mind or a communicate with a fellow passenger have been disrupted by way of way of car horns, billboards, or perhaps the radio on your vehicle.

When your mind divert your hobby from a message you are listening to or analyzing, that is referred to as mental noise. Imagine your agency emails you at four:forty five p.M. Soliciting for the profits records from the preceding month, an analysis of the modern-day-day income estimates, and the income figures from the identical month over the past 5 years. Your boss is in a meeting in a tremendous region. Opening the email and beginning to check it is able to make you decided, "Great—no problem—I even have the ones records and that evaluation proper right right here on my laptop." You supply a respond with the maximum modern-day predictions and the income facts from the previous month related. Afterward, you close up up down your computer and bypass domestic at 5 o'clock.

The subsequent morning, your supervisor calls and apologizes for the hassle due to your omission of the preceding 12 months's earnings records. What the difficulty turn out to be? Interference: You stored your self from studying cautiously enough to comprehend the whole of your boss's message with the useful useful resource of thinking about the manner you favored to reply.

There are many sources of interference as nicely. Your attention may be diverted by means of way of using hunger, making it hard as a way to concentrate. Perhaps it is hot and stuffy on the place of work. How may additionally moreover this affect your potential to pay interest and make contributions when you have been a participant in an target audience taking note of an executive speech?

Noise obstructs the message's normal encoding and interpreting at the channel maximum of the deliver and the receiver. While no longer all noise is bad, it hinders communication. For example, despite the fact that the sound of your cell telephone can be exciting to you, it may annoy your friends and disrupt beauty discussions.

Two Communication Models

When humans are speakme, the supply and the receiver also can both transmit messages on the equal time, often overlapping. You will regularly characteristic each the supply and the receiver even as speakme.

You'll address how the target market hears and is aware of your messages. The goal marketplace's reaction will take the form of remarks, with the intention to offer you with essential guidelines. Although there are unique conversation models, in this text we will cope with that provide insights and commands for company communicators.

Researchers regularly regard communique as a transactional manner (Figure 1, "Transactional Model of Communication"), with activities often taking place on the equal time, in area of seeing the deliver sending a message and someone receiving it as impartial acts. In conversational turn-taking, for instance, on the same time as each players carry out every roles simultaneously, the road among supply and receiver is blurred.

00001.Jpeg

Figure 1: Transactional Model of Communication

Researchers have moreover checked out the notion that every person creates our interpretations of the message. What I said and what you heard could not had been the identical, because the State Department quotation at the hollow of this bankruptcy shows. When attempting to outline communique, the constructivist model (Figure 2. "Constructivist Model of Communication") makes a speciality of the negotiated meaning, or common ground

Imagine consuming out for supper on the same time as on tour in Atlanta, Georgia. You can also say "positive" whilst requested whether or not or not or now not you would love a "Coke." When the waiter asks over again, "what kind," you can reply, "Coke is OK." What type of mild drink ought to you need, the waiter also can then ask a third time. This instance illustrates a commonplace false impression: most clean drinks in Atlanta, in which the Coca-Cola Company is located, are virtually called "Cokes."

Even in case you need to get a slight drink that isn't always a cola or possibly created via the Coca-Cola Company, you want to indicate the kind on the identical time as setting your order. The terms "pop," "soda pop," or "soda" can be more often used to offer an reason for a tender drink in numerous factors of the u . S . Than the brand "Coke." In this situation, the time period "Coke" is belief with the aid of every you and the waiter, but you have conflicting mind approximately what it method. To properly draw close the request and deliver a reaction, you should first create common ground and understand what the possibility character's interpretation of the word implies.

00002.Jpeg

Figure 2: Constructivist Model of Communication

We can make use of a dictionary to assist us whilst you keep in mind that we function the diverse meanings of words, gestures, and thoughts inner us, however we can despite the fact that need to negotiate what to intend.

The Final Word

The 8 crucial components of communication are the deliver, message, channel, receiver, remarks, environment, context, and interference. Communication consists of records, sharing, and this means that. The transactional way, in which sports activities take place simultaneously, and the constructivist version, which emphasizes shared this means that, are examples of communique fashions.

Chapter 7: Barriers to Effective Communication

There are numerous reasons for interpersonal people of the own family to move wrong. The message (what is uttered) may not continually be understood exactly because the sender intended. Therefore, the communicator want to invite for remarks to make sure that their message is comprehended.

Active listening, clarification, and reflected photo are useful communication techniques, however a notable communicator ought to furthermore be aware of the limitations to a success verbal exchange and apprehend a manner to get round or over them.

There are many limitations to communique, and they're able to seem at any thing inside the path of the exchange. You run the risk of squandering time and/or cash through the usage of producing uncertainty and misunderstanding because of the truth obstacles can also distort your message.

Overcoming those barriers and speakme a message this is clean and succinct are vital for effective verbal exchange.

Jargon use is a commonplace barrier to powerful verbal exchange. Complex, difficult to apprehend, or too convoluted terminology.

Taboos and emotional limitations. It may be tough for wonderful people to talk their feelings, and high-quality subjects might be honestly "off-limits" or taboo. Politics, religion, bodily and mental disability, sexuality and sex, racism, and any point of view that may be visible as unpopular are examples of taboo or tough topics.

Lack of hobby, diversions, lack of awareness, or receiver irrelevance (For similarly details, see our article on Obstacles to Effective Listening.)

Different perspectives and strategies of seeing.

Physical impairments like speakme impediments or paying attention to issues.

Objects that prevent nonverbal verbal exchange. Communication may be a whole lot much less a fulfillment if nonverbal clues, gestures, posture, and common frame language are not visible. Face-to-face contact is regularly greater a success than mobile phone calls, texts, and wonderful technology-based totally definitely verbal exchange techniques.

Language boundaries encompass problems in decoding accents from exquisite nations.

Expectations and biases that might result in inaccurate assumptions or stereotyping. People regularly concentrate what they assume to pay attention in choice to what's said and draw the wrong conclusions as a end result. For further information, see The Ladder of Inference on our internet net web page.

Cultural variations. In addition to the manner emotions are conveyed, social interaction requirements variety widely among cultures. The concept of personal place, for instance, differs at some point of cultures and among numerous social contexts. For further information, see our web page on intercultural sensitivity.

A ready communicator want to be aware of the ones limitations and artwork to lessen their have an impact on via frequently confirming comprehension and imparting beneficial comments.

Classification of conversation obstacles

Language Issues

Communication may additionally regularly be hampered by using way of problems with language and linguistic competence.

However, even if speaking in the identical language, a message's terminology might also function a barrier if the recipient does now not virtually understand it (s). For instance, a recipient who's strange with the language used will now not recognize a message that makes use of a whole lot of specialised jargon and abbreviations.

Regional slang and phrases run the danger of being misunderstood or maybe insulting. For further details, please go to our net page on powerful speakme.

Psychiatric Obstacles

The communicators' mental states may want to have an effect on how the message is transmitted, acquired, and interpreted.

For example:

Someone who is confused out may be distracted through non-public issues and less aware of the message than someone who isn't always careworn out.

We may additionally moreover moreover decorate our interpersonal interactions via way of studying the way to manipulate our stress. Another mental obstacle to communique is anger. It's easy to mention matters we may additionally moreover regret saying later even as we are furious, and it's also simple to misread what different people are announcing.

In state-of-the-art, human beings with bad vanity can be tons much less forceful and, as a surrender quit result, won't revel in comfortable talking out; they may be afraid to express their actual feelings out loud or interpret accidental horrible connotations in what others say.

Physical Obstacles

The physical scenario of the receiver also can offer physiological barriers to verbal exchange.

For instance, if there is a lot of facts noise, a receiver with impaired paying attention to won't be capable of certainly recognize what is being said in a spoken talk.

Physical Barriers

The geographical distance between the transmitter and recipient is an instance of a physical communique barrier (s).

Since there are extra communication channels to be had and much much less system is wanted, communication is frequently less difficult at shorter distances. Face-to-face communication is excellent.

Although present day technology regularly lessens the effect of bodily obstacles, it's miles though essential to understand the advantages and disadvantages of every communique channel to choose the first-rate one for disposing of the limitations.

Systematic Obstacles

In establishments and corporations wherein there are useless or inadequate information structures and communication channels, or while there may be a lack of expertise of the roles and obligations for communique, there may be systemic limitations to verbal exchange. People in those organizations might not be smooth on how they wholesome into the communique machine and what's anticipated of them as a give up give up result.

Attitudinal Barriers

Attitudinal boundaries are attitudes or behaviors that make it hard for people to talk truely.

Communication problems because of attitudes can be because of person problems, horrific leadership, reluctance to change, or a lack of ambition. You ought to make an effort to move over your intellectual obstacles to improve the effectiveness of communique.

Chapter 8: It all begins offevolved offevolved with Listening

A professional listener pays hobby to the speaker so that it will correctly pay attention and comprehend their terms. Nobody enjoys talking with someone honestly inquisitive about what they have to mention. Because of this, you must moreover be a excellent listener in case you want to turn out to be a first rate communicator.

What Do Communication Listening Skills Entail?

One of the fundamental smooth abilties is listening. It well-knownshows a person's functionality for statistics reception and interpretation within the direction of the communique.

Without the capability to actively pay attention, you may not be able to recognize what is being said. As a impact, there might be a conversation breakdown, and the speaker can also grow agitated very rapid.

How Well Can You Listen?

Particularly at paintings, it makes you feel particular and valued even as someone will be aware of what you need to offer. But have you ever ever ever considered that when you have sturdy listening skills?

Answer the subsequent inquiries to decide whether or not or not or no longer you're a excellent listener. Check to look whether or not you exercising:

Often interrupt others when they're speaking

Talk while others are speakme

Jump to conclusions prolonged earlier than the speaker is finished speaking

Often ask people to copy themselves

Let your feeling within the course of the speaker come among your listening capability.

If "YES" changed into your reaction to any of the aforementioned questions, you may need to paintings on honing your listening competencies.

The Value of Communication Skills in Listening

The functionality to pay attention is a key aspect of powerful communication. If you can effectively communicate, you can begin to decorate social and expert connections. Additionally, you may be able to decide greater efficiently and are available to an agreement with others extra speedy.

The following elements make listening abilties essential:

1. It lessens misunderstandings

Misunderstandings commonly stem from bad communique. Additionally, awful listening competencies cause bad communique. If people do no longer tell their issue of the story or actively pay attention to others, they land up making assumptions about every different and misinterpreting every other. As a result, mishearing or misinterpreting records is straightforward. If listening competencies in communique aren't superior, such misunderstandings also can additionally grade by grade hold growing.

2. Promotes Empathy

For taking note of benefit success, empathy is essential. So it might be better in case you in addition expressed the speaker's emotions. Your facial expressions and phrases need to reflect the speaker's feelings, along with melancholy or satisfaction, for instance. Empathy for the speaker requires recognition and exertion, which promotes connection building and open verbal exchange.

3. Sets Judgment Limits

Judgments are restrained whilst we pay interest. Your whole focus stays on the speaker on the identical time as you actively listen to them. To keep away from passing judgment on the alternative person or organization of human beings, you consequently make each attempt to understand them. As they're sharing their views with you, you need to consequently pay attention to what they've got to say with an open mind. As they stop the presentation, you may apprehend that the speech makes more revel in.

4. Strengthens Business Relations

Your ability to talk is critical on your achievement when you have a consumer-focused or interactive mission. Therefore, operating toward effective listening techniques with everyone at paintings allow you to be successful. You may also enhance your relationships together together together with your coworkers. Everyone will admire and respect you greater for this reason.

5. Boosts Productivity

At domestic or agency, listening is crucial in your success. People who pay interest nicely are much more likely to do not forget records and recognise what is anticipated of them. In institution tasks and conferences, that is a beneficial abilties. People can receive as proper with that to make contributions, they want to say masses, however listening is possibly extra critical. Misunderstandings are plenty a good deal much less probably to stand up if certainly every body may be aware about each unique. Everyone becomes greater productive as a give up result.

6. Strengthens Leadership Qualities

Leaders are usually incredible communicators who pay interest properly. You can connect with your group's thoughts, hear different factors of view, and avoid misunderstandings with the aid of actively listening. A prepared agency chief additionally makes pleasant that everyone feels favored, which makes all people experience heard. They continuously be privy to what others have to say and try to be of help.

7. Offering pointers

The simplest way to provide the speaker remarks is to actively be aware of them. The motive of feedback is to permit the speaker understand that you are paying hobby. Feedback can be vocal or nonverbal in type.

For vocal enter, you can use phrases like "good enough" or "I get it." Additionally, you could nod your head and use other appropriate facial expressions to offer nonverbal enter. It moreover demonstrates your interest to element in case you write down what the speaker says.

How Can You Develop Better Communication Listening Skills?

You must have a have a have a look at your listening talents to discover the areas that need to be superior. Here are a few tips to help you become higher at listening:

1. Continue to appearance the speaker in the eye

Always appearance the speaker in the attention whether or not or no longer in a hard and fast setting or in the direction of a speech. You are giving the speaker your entire hobby via doing this. Additionally, it demonstrates that you are attempting to understand what they will be announcing. The speaker will consequently experience as though their efforts are being valued.

Additionally, it conveys to them nonverbally your interest to what they've got to say, which conjures up them to keep speaking. As a prevent end result, you need to keep away from being sidetracked throughout conferences and public talking. You need to chorus from, as an instance:

Browsing through your cellphone or sending texts,

Viewing through a window,

A computer display experiment

Body language, including chewing your finger or raking it through your hair, is every extraordinary example.

The speaker from time to time fails to appearance the goal market in the eye. This is a result in their ability shyness or unease. Or that verbal exchange in their culture does no longer embody direct eye contact. Even inside the occasion that they do not glance at you, you need to keep going through the speaker.

2. Visualize the speaker's phrases.

When taking note of a topic, seeing some detail associated with it might assist you don't forget it. This will help you without trouble undergo in thoughts phrases and phrases on the equal time as you pay attention to the speaker. As a end end result, as you pay attention to the speaker, try to visualize what they may be announcing.

You can also additionally employ simple snap shots or locations related to the scenario to create a highbrow picture. However, in case you start to lose reputation at the same time as visualizing some problem, don't forget to return to it proper away.

3. Don't Disrupt

Each individual has a completely unique degree of information of a subject. For instance, you can now not apprehend all that a person says to you in numerous situations. To guide and supply an reason for the priority or time period you probably did no longer apprehend, you may choice to invite a question.

But earlier than you provide them a question, look forward to a lull in their speak. By doing so, you talk to the speaker which you are inquisitive about what they have got to mention and are open to more communicate. Additionally, the speaker will fee the opportunity to finish their announcement without interruption.

4. Take Note of Nonverbal Cues

Our number one form of communique is nonverbal. Without uttering a word, our frame language and voice tone regularly supply our emotions. Simply seeing the speaker's eyes, lips, and shoulders can also assist you to recognize if they may be fascinated, agitated, or excited.

Along with paying attention to the speaker, you need to be aware about how others are acting. It will make it much less tough as a way to apprehend what the individual speaking to you is making an attempt to deliver.

5. Exercise your being attentive to

Any capability can be improved and observed out with workout; listening includes being privy to what to do whilst a person is speakme to you. As a end end result, going for walks towards will help you emerge as better at listening. For instance, you need to summarize what you heard and comprehended and offer the speaker remarks in writing.

You also can be aware of podcasts or audiobooks, every of which may be outstanding for developing your listening abilties. However, you must no longer take note of a few factor longer than a 4-minute section. To determine how a bargain of the audio you had been able to hold, jot down what you recognize and playback the audio clip.

You may acquire new competencies with the beneficial resource of severa professional businesses, together with One Education.

The Final Word

Expressing hobby in the state of affairs being addressed and comprehending the records given are two signs and symptoms that one is listening well. A individual's capability to concentrate properly is important internal and out of the venture. People with sturdy listening abilities regularly get promoted or art work on obligations they decide on.

In the process, listening abilties provide a massive sort of advantages. Good listeners foster higher working relationships, growth output, and do one in all a type subjects. You have to first recognize why you are a horrific listener to enhance your listening skills. Work on your shortcomings after that.

Chapter 9: Giving better response

Whether you're answering questions after a presentation, collaborating in a TV interview, or replying to thoughts in the course of a assembly, the language and messaging you use are vital.

Your phrases have a big effect on how others see you. They have an impact on how others understand you.

In most interpersonal interactions, the effect of your messages is matched through how well you can actively concentrate and ask insightful questions.

But in terms of efficaciously react to their remarks, you'll have the gain if you have a deep popularity of different humans and decide what makes them tick.

Your interactions turns into more potent as you get higher at spotting and comprehending man or woman trends. Because you may continuously experience in control, your government presence and air of gravity and authority may be strengthened.

While lively listening is crucial in Q&A lessons and media interviews, it's far as critical to expose that you have the cognitive capability to choose the proper phrases at the ideal second to bring the favored message.

We will teach you the way to assist your intellectual questioning at the equal time as you bear in mind a manner to react to even the maximum difficult queries. Thinking speedy and correctly in your ft calls for big knowledge.

What are the right reactions for healthful interpersonal communication?

Healthy interpersonal communique calls for replies which might be regarded as being sympathetic, kind, heat, and thoughtful.

The following eight answers are looked after from maximum a success to least effective

Understanding

Clarification

Self Disclosure

Questioning

Information Giving

Reassurance

Analytical

Advice Giving

But preserve in thoughts that relying on the state of affairs, any of those reactions may be appropriate.

Review all the responses, specifically the examples. Which reactions are most possibly to foster a wonderful interpersonal dynamic?

Understanding

The risk that an facts response will foster open, honest communication is excessive. It is an emotional response that demonstrates sensitivity and comprehension. Strong terrible emotions might save you people from talking; this response can lessen such sentiments.

Empathy, or precisely tuning in to what the other individual is experiencing within the advocate time, is just like facts. It shows being attentive to past the spoken word and expressing emotions.

Responses that advise expertise;

You're feeling defeated and wondering what the aspect is.

You're enraged and outraged.

Your new challenge has you all fired up.

You appear pleased that you were selected.

By focused on unique human beings's feelings, you renowned that they're precise folks that need your care. Normal people's angry sentiments may be lessened thru way of this form of response. When a person can be very emotional, sobbing, afraid, and so forth., it can additionally be implemented to assist them get over those emotions or behaviors.

Clarification

Your choice to recognize what the other person is saying or to pinpoint the most important sentiments which might be manifesting is shown via your clarifying solution. It implies which you value what others have to say and are verifying it to affirm your perspectives. This can be done in severa processes, which include via using paraphrasing, summarizing, or repeating the last few terms spoken. A time of quiet can be used productively after this sort of reaction. This offers the others an possibility to make a contribution mind or refute your perception. Your preference to take a look at topics from a few other character's mind-set is bolstered with the resource of clarification answers.

Clarification replies examples:

I count on that in advance than the birth of your infant, you have got got been capable of control your marriage.

You look like expressing the choice to move back to California and indicating that you have been glad there.

Let's see, do you choice to search for a career that offers greater mission?

You are declaring that you may provide you with a higher method of undertaking this if I understand you proper.

This response is strong in lowering antagonism. When you observe it with quiet, it no longer simplest persuades the others to problematic extra but additionally allows to keep the conversation on track. It offers the opportunity humans an possibility to set up their thoughts and take ownership of growing with their necessities. Responding with a request for explanation additionally can be used as a time-purchasing for tactic on the identical time as you hold in thoughts a better answer.

Self-Disclosure

Self-disclosure demonstrates your efforts to let others realise extra approximately who you are. It includes revealing some component about oneself that is pertinent to the discourse, which includes your values, views, or in advance revel in. By letting humans apprehend they're not by myself in their emotions or anxieties, self-disclosure may additionally assist humans enjoy an awful lot much less demanding.

Self-disclosure response examples:

The health practitioner additionally handled us the manner at the equal time as we delivered our son!

I've constantly belief it have end up terrific to be silent at the identical time as my parents were arguing.

Like you, I in no manner had the effect that all of us trendy me actually as I have emerge as.

Kids used to tease me approximately my weight and the clothing I wore once I changed into more youthful, so I am acquainted with what it's far like to paste out in a crowd.

Self-disclosure permits installation a reference to someone who shares your demanding situations or problems in life. In helping relationships, this reassures the helpees that they're in the proper location and that others spherical them have faced comparable issues. Utilizing this reaction too regularly draws interest to the incorrect character, which isn't useful. It is probably visible as a method of drawing interest. To have the best impact, use minimally.

Questioning

The inquiry reaction's motive is to elicit information, definitely how it sounds. It lets in others to difficult on a topic. Open-ended inquiries focus on the broader times, thoughts, emotions, and responses of the other character. They frequently inspire communique. Closed inquiries frequently elicit a certain or no response and give attention to fantastic information or tendencies of the alternative person's situation.

Examples of answers to questions

Do you and your business enterprise organization get alongside nicely? Can you tell me about your boss? (Closed) Do you need the trendy home? (open) What do you recognize approximately the ultra-modern-day house? (Closed) (open) Do you discover this complicated? What exactly are you confused approximately? (open)

Open-ended inquiries are recommended whilst analyzing a massive state of affairs. Closed-ended questions is probably blanketed to skip to precise information or to surrender extended, useless lectures. In each scenario, it's miles vital to the wondering technique to be aware of the reaction, each what is said and what is left unsaid. Questions that begin with why have to be approached with warning. They can engender resentment through pressuring the alternative person for a evidence. Questions approximately why would likely come out as being essential or lessen down, seeming to signify disdain.

Information Giving

Giving data consists of impartially relaying information with out opinion or evaluation. The special man or woman is unfastened to agree or disagree with the statistics. It allows the opportunity to anticipate obligation for making use of the statistics. Giving every correct and terrible feedback with this technique (struggle of phrases). The others clearly communicate to what has happened and the consequences which have resulted from it.

Words like commonly, in no manner, need to, and ought are absolutely hired to set up obstacles. (The specifics of what need to or must no longer be completed, as well as cut-off dates and policies.)

Examples of solutions that provide records

These schooling may also moreover last up to 12 weeks, however they ought with a view to address your requirements.

Every little one needs to be touched and nurtured to growth up feeling worth.

The aid group may be applied to connect to others going thru similar problems.

Responding to others' sentiments with an knowledgeable answer will increase the danger in their respecting and obeying the regulations recommended.

Reassurance

Responses that offer guarantee calm human beings down, disperse robust feelings and display self perception. They pat themselves on the once more however suggest that effective feelings or thoughts are OK due to the fact they may be not unusual or normal. Due to its propensity to lessen others' worries, this response does no longer sell interpersonal relationships. This agency consists of clichés. People, who encounter a scenario that is outside in their experience range sometimes flip to reassurance because of the reality they may be uncertain of what to do or say and might enjoy humiliated. ?

Examples of reassuring feedback

Not to fear. You might be victorious because of the truth others have in advance than you.

It may also appear horrible right now, but the entirety is probably OK inside the morning.

You aren't obese.

Welcome to life after a calamity due to the fact the "new everyday."

Hold at once to choice. Being dissatisfied is a not unusual emotion.

To be more successful, this reaction might be rephrased as an data, clarifying, or information-giving reaction. When combined with other reactions, used as a signal of compassion, it is probably useful. For instance, use "You have managed this problem previously" in area of "You will control." Unwind and use warning. I agree with in you, consequently I inspire you to do what appears proper to you (reassurance).

Analytical

To take a look at, offer an reason behind, or understand the alternative man or woman's behavior and feelings is the purpose of the analytical response. It goes in addition than what the other has stated to link or provide an motive for ideas and occurrences. This reaction, in assessment to explanation, consists of a few trouble out of your thoughts, emotions, values, and plenty of others. It suggests that you are informed and superior to the alternative individual. The analytical technique regularly motives others to come to be resentful.

Illustrations of analytical answers

He makes you recollect you studied of your estranged father, it really is why you are having this type of difficult time with him.

You frequently arrive overdue for our appointments due to the fact you do no longer revel in at home proper here.

Because you notice her as a leader, you discover it tough to empathize collectively with her.

You are by myself due to the fact you are hesitant to take a chance on making friends.

When there can be an ongoing counseling connection and the affected person wishes to be made privy to powerful behavior or response patterns, the analytical reaction is more perfect for therapists.

Even nevertheless, there are situations whilst an answer that gives records is finest. Analytical is a terrible response to appoint at the equal time as bringing up someone's want to enhance their conduct.

Advice Giving

Giving advice often has little advantage. It shows which you are in a function to apprehend the reasons of the problems of various human beings and what they want to, want to, or ought to do to clear up them. As a result, you're evaluating the morality, propriety, standard overall performance, or accuracy of the others' deeds. By the requirements of your precise fee tool, others are visible to be somehow poor. This is a way of assigning blame for one's problems.

Examples of feedback that provide recommendation

I'd write to him and beg him to present you a few factor for the children if I had been you. The first-class manner to treatment your marriage troubles is to acquire a divorce.

Instead of arguing, try to understand the opportunity man or woman's factor of view.

You want to no longer talk within the shape of manner.

When someone is suggested what to do, they may be not in fee of creating alternatives or resolving troubles. Even at the identical time as there can be apparent conformity, recommendation frequently meets with resistance and hostility. Even even as sought, giving recommendation could probably encourage reliance. Convert advice right right into a question or a solution that gives information.

How is empathy communicated?

To reply healthily, one ought to display empathy, or the capacity to apprehend.

Reflection, which serves as a mirror and offers feedback, is a beneficial approach for expressing empathy. Reflection demonstrates comprehension of the emotional content material of what's spoken in addition to the encircling factors (sports having an impact on the feelings expressed).

Being aware about others' dreams allows you to get insightful comments that permits you speak more successfully. A high-quality, respectful sensation of being heard and understood develops at the same time as others agree with that what they've got to say and how they feel is profitable.

This bond strengthens the assisting dating's foundation of agree with and encourages mission motivation.

Additionally, you may react as it have to be as you develop greater attuned to others' desires. Reflecting empathy is giving a thoughtful response at the equal time as the use of every other language to speak the authentic cause.

Reflective Empathy Example

Other: I'm no longer honestly into the ones gadgets proper now. I do now not understand any of the scientific jargon you are the usage of, therefore I couldn't supply a rattling about it. My child has issues, and I am conscious that I am getting a raw deal.

You: Learning new phrases may be stressful and nerve-wracking, in particular because of the reality you did not request any of this.

Other: Okay, so if you may just supply an reason for to me what I want to do to help him.

Reflective remarks need to be aim without passing judgment. A judgemental answer adjustments the which means that of the opportunity individual's statements, gives a cutting-edge forestall, or characterizes their movements as particular or evil.

For instance:

Other: I'm not certain. It's actually no longer what I speculated to have a toddler. I believed it would growth my level of arousal and make existence extra interesting. However, it seems like my circle of relatives life is at a standstill. My hubby and I land up doing not anything except lounging spherical. With a kid, our marriage has exceeded thru a full-size change.

Poor mirrored photograph of judgment: Too horrible you experience unmoving. If you probably did not simply sit down down round, it could be interesting.

(This contradicts the speaker and is prejudicial; it does now not show that you listened to the speaker.)

Good non judgmental mirrored photo: You declare that having a infant hasn't added approximately the sparkling and interesting change to your marriage which you had was hoping for.

Advice on a way to react to human beings to have a cordial cooperative connection

1. React in a manner that draws hobby to the problems and concerns; element out contradictions and immediately and discretely accumulate records.

2. Express to the opposite man or woman that you are paying interest and taking in what they may be pronouncing. Donate sometimes. I see, or yeah, okay.

three. To elicit similarly information, use open-ended questions. Use Tell me extra about..., Let's communicate it, or I simply have a query regarding... It is typically greater a achievement to respond in this manner than through manner of asking precise who, what, even as, in which, and why inquiries.

4. Request rationalization, as an example, through expressing "I'm not facts what you are saying." Is it this...? Or Could you kindly skip over it all over again?

5. Clear Use of language. To decide the alternative individual's comprehension diploma, be aware about their terminology.

6. Try not to lecture, detail arms, or be obnoxious.

7. Make an attempt to live on mission rely.

eight. Respond with honesty and empathy to allow the opportunity person feel cushty citing greater facts.

9. Strive to avoid speakme too much approximately your self. Limit your self-disclosure.

10. React in a way that is appropriate for the opportunity character's age, sex, and emotional condition.

eleven. Steer clear of feedback that make you appear protective. I make an apology; I did not intend to use this kind of poor technique.

12. Feel relaxed in quiet. Do no longer feel that quiet ought to be damaged thru communique. Don't chat all of the time.

13. Aim to be impartial and nonjudgmental at the same time as responding to behaviors, feedback, or conditions that you find out offensive, startling, or confrontational.

14. Aim to get the communique back at the proper music in case you start to burst off situation.

15. Allow parents to weep in the occasion that they experience emotional. Be respectful. While you do not need to save you them from sobbing, do your top notch to lead them to enjoy relaxed.

sixteen. Make eye contact, lean forward, and use receptive body language.

Chapter 10: Before you communicate, Listen

To speak successfully, you want to first pay attention. Messages are readily misconstrued if one lacks the skill to pay hobby successfully. As a give up cease result, there may be a breakdown in conversation, and the message sender also can furthermore emerge as upset or dissatisfied. Because listening is so essential, many prestigious companies offer their body of workers with listening capabilities schooling. This isn't surprising for the reason that powerful listening skills can bring about higher productivity with fewer errors, better client happiness, advanced records sharing, and in the end extra imaginitive and innovative paintings. Many successful businesspeople and leaders attribute their fulfillment to their capability to pay attention efficaciously.In the verbal exchange approach, listening is the capability to as it should be pay attention and interpret communications.

All successful interpersonal connections are built at the capability to pay interest efficaciously.Think about and paintings on improving your listening abilties due to the fact they'll be the muse of fulfillment.

Our personal lives can also advantage from having specific listening abilities. These benefits consist of getting extra pals and social networks, feeling extra confident and self-confident, getting higher grades in class and on assignments, or maybe playing higher fitness and normal properly-being. According to investigate, listening cautiously can decrease blood stress, at the identical time as speakme can increase it.

Hearing isn't just like listening. Hearing The noises that attain your ears are referred to as "paying attention to." It is a bodily machine that, if you do no longer have any listening to issues, takes place with out your aware awareness. But listening requires extra than just that—it calls for focus and awareness, each intellectual and sometimes physical. Listening consists of listening to the tale being told further to the manner wherein it's far being added, in addition to the speaker's use of language, voice, and frame language. It consists of being aware about each verbal and nonverbal cues. The quantity to which you apprehend and understand this information will determine how nicely you may pay interest.

The act of listening is not passive. In truth, the audience member can also and ought to take part within the tool at the least as actively due to the fact the speaker. This technique of giving your complete interest is referred to as "active listening." To completely and effectively recognise the speaker's thoughts and thing of view.

To evaluate what is being said severely.

To higher keep near what is being stated by way of paying interest To the nonverbal cues that go along with it.

To exhibit interest, consideration, and cognizance.

Encourage the speaker to express themselves surely, in fact, and openly.

To exercising being selfless and placing the speaker first.

To reach a together suitable know-how of every factors' factors of view.

When we're listening, growing with responses is regularly our top priority. This has not some thing to do with listening. To nicely apprehend the speaker, we want to take the time to pay close to interest to every what's being stated and the manner it is being stated.

Concentration and using your certainly one of a kind senses, in addition to being attentive to what's being said, are vital for effective listening.

training of listening talents

Educative listeningListening selectivelyListening with biascompassionate hearingfull-spectrum listeningTherapeutic or sympathetic

Listening for data You will utilize informational being attentive to recognize and undergo in mind facts on the same time as you need to observe some factor.

To conduct this form of listening, a excessive degree of recognition is generally required. That's because of the reality studying a modern undertaking depend calls for some of awareness. Additionally, you need to use vital questioning to analyze what you are reading. This is finished so that you can realise what you are reading within the mild of pertinent statistics. Informational listening includes, as an instance: art work revel in Self-paced education at art work or domestic eating an instructive audiobook Coaching Knowing the manner to employ informational listening offers you the energy to improve your studying. Your ability to actively observe and increase your self will make you a extra precious worker.

can also experience more content material fabric after they test their passions and select out up new abilties at domestic.

Listening with prejudice The first listening style you're born with is discriminative listening.

Everyone is born with the potential to concentrate carefully.This form of being attentive to is used even earlier than you may understand speech. Discriminative listening is based totally an lousy lot a good deal much less on terms and extra on verbal cues, adjustments in voice tone, and distinctive sounds. Before they may apprehend phrases, newborns use a manner known as discriminative listening to decide the which means of a word. They will smile and snigger in reaction if a person speaks to them in a happy and pleased manner.

Because they could distinguish amongst wonderful voices, they can also discover who is speakme.However, taking note of with difference is not simply a toddler element.Your discriminative listening capabilities will probable be used mechanically if you're being attentive to a communicate being spoken in a far off locations language.These will can help you apprehend what is being said with the aid of the usage of studying tone and inflection. Nonverbal cues also may be used for listening and assessment. For instance, you can analyze lots approximately someone's message from their facial expressions, frame language, and extraordinary behavior.

Even if you could apprehend someone's language, discriminative listenng stays vital.Understanding the nuances of a discourse calls for this shape of listening. You can discover ways to study among the strains and pay interest what is being stated with the aid of the usage of this listening abilties.

Here's an instance:Consider asking considered one in all your coworkers whether or not they concur with a path of movement.They verify, however you can tell there is a problem based on their body language, which encompass after they bypass uncomfortably.You can choose up on this with the aid of listening carefully, in which case you need to inquire approximately their degree of fact. You can also inquire as to whether or no longer they would like topics to appear.

Listening bias, Selective listening is each other name for biased listening. Biased listeners best be aware about the statistics they expressly need to pay interest. This listening technique has the capacity to skew the fact. This takes place due to the reality the listener isn't always virtually tuned into what the speaker is trying to mention.Here's an instance:Imagine that your boss is explaining a contemporary venture to you. You're disturbing to examine the specifics of this assignment due to the fact you have been looking ahead to it for a while.

You do not absolutely be aware of what your supervisor says since you're so preoccupied with the specifics of the task. You pay attention your boss describe how you may be evaluated on this task, but you do not completely recognize what they may be saying.

Compassionate listening, The motivation for sympathetic listening is emotion. The listener concentrates at the speaker's feelings and emotions in preference to the message conveyed through terms. To technique the ones feelings and emotions, that is achieved.You can offer the speaker the help they want with the useful useful resource of using sympathetic listening. Not what they claim to be feeling, but how they genuinely sense, is some issue you may understand.When you make the effort to pay attention on this way, the speaker will experience heard and tested.If you need to boom a stronger courting with a person for your existence, listening with empathy is vital. Let's say, as an instance, which you run proper into a coworker on the grocery hold. You decide to be privy to them due to the reality they seem upset, so you do.To recognize how human beings are feeling, you may additionally hire empathetic listening. In

Thorough listening Comprehensive listening necessitates language knowledge in assessment to discriminative taking note of. Early infancy is commonly while this kind of listening is fashioned.To recognize what's being said verbally, human beings want entire listening abilties.Other listening techniques enlarge on thorough listening. For instance, that allows you to use informational listening and check something new, comprehensive listening is wanted. You'll probable lease a mixture of whole and discriminative listening to interpret the alerts that humans are offering you to your life and at paintings. Consider the situation in which a colleague informs you of a project. To study the phrases and recognise the this means that that, you need to listen carefully. When you get hold of comments, you could also pay attention cautiously.

Compassionate or recovery listeningIt's beneficial to pay interest with empathy if you want to understand distinct human beings's viewpoints.When listening in this way, you could take some time to apprehend the attitude of the speaker. Attempting to place oneself in the one-of-a-kind person's footwear is any other possibility. You can hire sympathetic listening to relate to someone else's research as even though they were your private, in area of definitely that specialize in their message.This is awesome from listening with empathy.You attempt to understand a person's emotions via empathetic listening with the intention to offer manual. However, you do no longer constantly try to envision how it might sense to be in their shoes.

Here's an illustration:Let's recall your boss surely knowledgeable you that the organization day trip this week has been postponed due to finances guidelines.

You can decide how a whole lot stress your manager is below through listening with empathy. You can picture your self having to deliver the disappointing statistics. You are aware that there can be pressure from above to stick to the rate variety. Additionally, you are conscious that there can be body of workers pressure. In location of buying. You're dissatisfied, but you could see why your manager made this choice. That's because of the fact you can picture what it'd be like for them to be to your function proper now.

Crucial hearings You'll want to lease critical listening in case you need to research complicated material.Deeper listening is viable whilst crucial concept is used while listening. Use vital listening to analyze what's being said in region of accepting it at face fee. When settling problems at work, attentive listening is crucial. You might likely make use of this type of listening, for example, at the same time as determining the manner to answer to an uncommon or complicated consumer request. This capability is crucial to evaluate amazing humans's recommendations and determine whether or not or now not or no longer you concur.You do not high-quality want to pay attention what they're pronouncing to do that. Additionally, you must hold in thoughts the larger photograph and evaluation your know-how with it.

Learn all types of paying attention to beautify your nice of life and profession.There isn't any superior listening technique. Instead, those seven types of listening complement one another to beautify your comprehension of the assets you listen.Being an fantastic listener will help you speak extra correctly, save you misunderstandings, and make learning new records less tough.

There are many brilliant reasons to pay hobby, and which one you need to have is based upon at the state of affairs and the person of the speech.Should pay near hobby to the messages being conveyed, putting apart outside distractions and assumptions.

Learn all sorts of taking note of enhance your superb of lifestyles and career.It is not viable to emphasize the value of listening.

The capability to pay attention nicely thru loads of listening competencies is genuinely as essential for communique as analyzing to specific what you need to say. It can not handiest assist you in processing facts on numerous ranges, however it is able to additionally facilitate social interaction. This is just so listening would possibly flow into beyond simply listening to.Additionally, it includes plenty extra than most effective paying attention to what others are announcing. Even even though this shape of listening is essential, it is not the satisfactory type.Let's talk about the numerous styles of listening and why it's miles critical for your private and professional development. Why is listening crucial in each day via way of day lifestyles and the place of job? A critical part of accurate conversation is listening.

Whatever the state of affairs, listening is crucial to comprehending what unique human beings are truely trying to talk. Without paying interest, it is easy to misinterpret and assume.

On the opportunity hand, you can truely talk with a person at the equal time as you surely listen.

The maximum essential aspect of communication is listening. This is because of the fact that it lets in you to boom a robust and large answer. With frame language especially, you can select out up on subtleties that you otherwise won't have.

You have the proper to make smooth something if crucial. Without lively listening, you may

Chapter 11: The self attention

The capability to understand and understand the characteristics that outline your particular character, inclusive of your moves, values, ideals, feelings, and thoughts, is referred to as self-hobby. It is largely a psychological state of affairs in which the self takes middle degree. Self-interest is an ongoing method in which a person learns more and more approximately their character abilities, strengths, feel of purpose, fundamental values, ideals, and desires. We can higher recognize our strengths and weaknesses thru taking character checks. Since they spend their days inside the the front of audiences, audio gadget need to have a higher enjoy of self. Self-aware humans are privy to their values. They realize what's critical to them and what hints they stay with the aid of way of manner of. This want to also ring real to the audio system. An actual presenter may be extra credible than one which does now not firmly believe in what they will be announcing.

People with a experience of self "apprehend their passions."Being obsessed on what you do demonstrates a immoderate degree of self-attention. The identical is real for public speaking experts. To communicate in self belief to strangers approximately who you're and what you want requires a lot of self notion. Those who make a dwelling from it have this ardour for what they do.

People who are aware of themselves "understand their aspirations." Knowing what you need out of lifestyles is a critical problem of self-focus. Setting extended-time period objectives is remarkable for your existence in addition on your message. You can clear up to hold your message everyday for months—or perhaps years—when you have aspirations. Your target market will come to consider you more due to your consistency. Adopt the surroundings in which you thrive. What sorts of environmental factors aid us in keeping our power? This may be determined for public talking using our badge assessment. Do you perform better in a boardroom or an area? Do massive crowds energize or drain you? Your universal performance is induced thru the ones person options. To make a stronger impact, pick out the right placing to your presentation. Speaking in public Self-aware humans understand "reactions," which refers to our fleeting reactions and the strengths and weaknesses contained therein. Professionals in public talking should be aware of their audience's cues. Analyze the emotions that your intention marketplace has expressed in reaction in your paintings if you are not glad. Getting comments may be very critical! Your target marketplace can offer beneficial comments on a way to make your presentation better.

People who're self-aware are aware about "the effect we've were given on others." We all obviously have an impact on specific people. Our actions have a massive kind of effects on people's lives, whether or now not or no longer at work, at home, or inside the community. The vital reason of presenters is to make a long-lasting effect that motivates motion. The stop of your presentation must continuously comprise a call to motion. Which motion do you need your target audience to take? With that as the focus of your presentation, quit thru the usage of soliciting for it.

A sort of cognitive-behavioral tactics that take area in each day existence are supported through self-consciousness. Because self-cognizance consists of a huge type of "corollaries," which include self-worth, self-assessment, strength of mind, self-aware feelings, self-efficacy, a revel in of business enterprise, the idea of mind, and self-speak. The author contends that self-reputation is important for some of behaviors, which consist of self-law, which refers to changing one's conduct, resisting temptation, or filtering out inappropriate data, despite the fact that this declare is not supported thru clinical proof. In order to bring about those cognitive-behavioral adjustments, we ought to be aware about what factors of ourselves want to be altered. An actual example is probably listening to from a member of the family which you regularly communicate over others and fail to pay interest at the same time as others are talking. Your self-interest has improved as a cease end result, and you could now consciously manipulate your behavior to avoid talking over special people. Being gift with yourself and your feelings can be practiced in lots of strategies, that can decorate yourself-popularity. Five seconds Meditation in reality looking at what takes region within the direction of a meditation can increase recognition of your mind and feelings. Meditation may be a mainly useful exercise because of the reality you do no longer have to worry approximately changing a few element. Perhaps you have got placed which you clench your jaw to hold tension in your frame or that it's far hard on the way to be in the gift second due to the truth you regularly fear approximately the destiny. You can observe extra about your self and your dispositions by way of manner of taking into consideration all of this beneficial facts.

Journaling Self-mirrored image bodily video games like journaling assist you to grow to be more aware about your dispositions in notion and conduct in addition to the areas of your lifestyles that you would possibly need to expand. Gaining an expertise of your lifestyles's testimonies and relationships may be restoration. Speaking Therapy The aim of remedy, along side cognitive behavioral remedy, is that will help you alternate unhelpful idea styles or behaviors.

For instance, you may be better capable of regulate your horrific mind and transfer to healthful coping mechanisms if you realise what is absolutely inflicting them.

Building emotional intelligence

Self-interest and emotional quotient (EQ) flow into collectively. The term "emotional intelligence" (EQ) describes a person's capability to recognize each their own emotions and people of others. Effective emotional responses may be made with empathy and compassion through someone with a immoderate EQ. !!BOf path, no person is wonderful, and EQ is only some one of a kind talent. However, you moreover mght help to increase your private self-hobby thru developing wholesome emotional expression for your self and energetic listening competencies on your interpersonal interactions.

Self-Consciousness People every so often will be predisposed to end up overly self-aware and err closer to self-focus. In some situations, this expanded self-recognition ought to make you feel uneasy and stressful.

These fleeting self-conscious feelings often appear even as we're "inside the highlight" and are quality short. However, for a few people, immoderate self-attention may be a symptom of a continual contamination like social anxiety disease.

Although self-interest is important for the manner we recognize ourselves, how we relate to others, and the manner we have interaction with the arena, immoderate self-interest can cause issues like anxiety and pressure.

degrees of consciousness

Public self-popularity: being privy to our capability public personas We are much more likely to conform with social norms and act in strategies which can be applicable in society because of this attention. Although this form of recognition has blessings, it additionally includes the threat of overt self-focus. People with excessive ranges of this trait may additionally fear excessively approximately what different human beings reflect onconsideration on them. Being able to understand and do not forget one's internal nation is called "personal self-recognition."

Private self-aware humans are introspective and approach their emotions and responses with interest.

For instance, you may seize your self tensing up as you get prepared for a vital meeting. Private self-attention might also look like noticing your physical signs and efficaciously attributing them for your assembly anxiety. We end up reluctant to show sure factors of ourselves whilst self-consciousness turns into self-attention. We create a individual this is untrue.

www.ingramcontent.com/pod-product-compliance
Lightning Source LLC
Chambersburg PA
CBHW071331120626
46546CB00002B/520